THE NEW
NO-PILL, NO-RISK
BIRTH CONTROL

✿❧✿❧✿❧✿❧✿

THE NEW
NO-PILL, NO-RISK
BIRTH CONTROL

❂❂❂❂❂❂❂

Nona Aguilar

❂❂❂❂❂❂❂

RAWSON ASSOCIATES : New York

"If I have seen further . . . it is by standing upon the shoulders of Giants." —SIR ISAAC NEWTON

To Edward F. Keefe, M.D. and Rudolf F. Vollman, M.D. Many have seen further; most have stood on their shoulders. —N.A.

Library of Congress Cataloging in Publication Data

Aguilar, Nona.
  The new no-pill, no-risk birth control.

  Includes bibliography and index.
  1. Rhythm method (Birth control). 2. Ovulation—
Detection. 3. Cervix mucus. 4. Body temperature—
Measurement. 5. Menstrual cycle. 6. Fertility, Human.
I. Title. [DNLM: 1. Contraception—methods—popular
works. 2. Family Planning—popular works. 3. Fertility—
popular works. WP 630 AP83n]
RG136.5.A38   1986   613.9′434   85-42927
ISBN 0-89256-299-4
ISBN 0-89256-300-1 (pbk.)

Published simultaneously in Canada by Collier Macmillan Canada, Inc.
Packaged by Rapid Transcript
Composition by Folio Graphics Co., Inc.

Designed by Jacques Chazaud

Printed and bound by Fairfield Graphics, Fairfield, Pennsylvania

First Edition

With the exception of Figure 8.1, which was reproduced with the permission of Linacre Laboratories, the illustrations in this book are by Cathy Kenneally, reproduced with the permission of Providence Hospital Natural Family Planning Program, Holyoke, Massachusetts

Contents

v

Foreword

❖❖❖❖❖❖❖❖

This book describes an effective birth control method that requires no drugs, chemicals, or barrier devices. There is only one requirement for its use: understanding.

Although the subject of reproduction has been studied for centuries, information on the cyclic levels of the reproductive hormones in serum during the menstrual cycle was first published only ten years ago. Since then, research concerning the pituitary, ovary, and their end-organs has been published at a fantastic rate. Possibly greater than 90 percent of the total volume of information on reproduction has been published in just this last decade. This information boom is becoming difficult for even the experts to handle.

That's why one of the things that most impresses me about this book is the author's ability to make biological and scientific facts clear and understandable. The extensive description of the many methods that measure the variables during the reproductive cycle is necessary and well done. The discussion and use of anecdotes to explain the results of these methods are easy to follow and understand. The section on nursing, which was a lost art for a time, is very informative for new parents. Indeed, as I read this book I kept wondering why we in academia, and the scientific community at large, can't seem to be able to impart information on reproduction as clearly and as concisely as the author does.

But besides the clarity of her presentation, Nona Aguilar has done an excellent job of asking the relevant questions. I am often amazed that many in the so-called sophisticated world of academic research are content merely with answers. They refuse to recognize that we desperately need good questions as well; such questions are the foundation of a better understanding of reproduction. In this regard, *No-Pill, No-Risk Birth Control* is a good,lesson to all. Miss Aguilar is able to show readers the whole forest, and at the same time knows how to examine the various trees calmly. This is obviously in contradistinction to some who hurry to examine the veins in a leaf but have limited interest in the nature of the tree and no interest whatsoever in the forest.

Throughout this foreword I have constantly focused my attention on reproduction. The reason is obvious: The relevant information is applicable to both the fertile and the infertile couple. But I can't stress the word *couple* enough. When both the man and the woman learn about the physiology of the reproductive system, there is an important basis for better understanding between them. It is this larger area of understanding that Nona Aguilar addresses particularly well.

Before concluding, I want to point out that my reading in the area of human reproduction is almost exclusively limited to medical journals, monographs, and reports on ongoing research. But I can say that I feel fortunate that a set of strange and wonderful circumstances brought this book my way.

1980   ROBERT M. NAKAMURA
Department of Obstetrics and Gynecology
University of Southern California Medical Center
Los Angeles, California

In reading the revised edition of this book, I was particularly pleased that Nona Aguilar was aware of Professor R. V. Short's significant discovery regarding the importance of breastfeeding-on-demand to maintain the infertile period after childbirth. Dr. Short's finding not only allows us to reconsider the importance of the 24-hour cycle as it relates to endocrine function but it has helped us to understand why our modern way of allowing the baby to sleep the whole night has eliminated the period of post-partum lactation infertility.

Although I have commented on only one section, the rest of the book has been gently modified to take into account new research findings. This is why readers of the first edition will find *The New No-Pill, No-Risk Birth Control* worth reading.

1986   ROBERT M. NAKAMURA

Acknowledgments

This book and its predecessor, *No-Pill, No-Risk Birth Control,* owe their existence to Maxine J. Lewis, who was health editor of *Family Circle* magazine until her retirement. It was Maxine who realized that there would be psychological ramifications of using a natural method of birth control and urged me to look into the difference they would make in a couple's relationship. That difference, combined with the high reliability of this new natural method, is the spur that made me want to write this book.

Others that made it possible include: Lester B. Anderman, M.D.; Kathleen Barrett, of Providence Hospital, Holyoke, Massachusetts; Mary Conroy, R.N., of St. Margaret's Hospital, Dorchester, Massachusetts; Carman and Jean Fallace, authors of *The Joy in Planning Your Family* (private printing); Virginia D. Gager; Edward F. Keefe, M.D.; Bonnie Manion, R.N.; Robert M. Nakamura, Ph.D., of the University of Southern California Medical Center; and Helen Paul, R.N., of Holy Name Hospital, Teaneck, New Jersey.

Important research information was provided by Lawrence Kane; John F. Kippley, director of the Couple to Couple League (Cincinnati, Ohio) and coauthor (with his wife, Sheila Kippley) of one of the most comprehensive books in the field, *The Art of Natural Family Planning;* Paul Marx, O.S.B., Ph.D.; Josef Roetzer, M.D.; and Gloria Roberts, of the Katherine Dexter McCormick Library of the Planned Parenthood World Population Information and Education Department.

Many portions of this book are informed by the valuable insights of James Fox, M.D., George M. Maloof, M.D., and

Herbert Ratner, M.D. In addition, I have received valuable advice from Marian J. Amft, Mary Louise Frawley, Charles G. Mills, and Paul C. Vitz, Ph.D., professor of psychology at New York University.

Others who deserve mention and thanks are Farley Clinton, Larry E. Huckins, Ph.D., Nancie Huckins, Robert A. Jonas, Ph.D., Carl B. McGowan, Ph.D., Evelyn Birge Vitz, Ph.D., Mary Shivanandan, and David Wilkinson, Ph.D.

Intelligent suggestions from Toni Sciarra, who helped edit this book, and from Sharon Morgan, who edited its predecessor, inform much of this work. I am grateful for the professional care and attention they gave to the respective manuscripts.

With the exception of figure 8.1, which was provided by Linacre Laboratories and reproduced with permission, all the drawings are by Cathy Kenneally and are available for purchase as a slide series from Providence Hospital Natural Family Planning Program in Holyoke, Massachusetts, which granted permission for their use.

I owe special thanks to hundreds of men and women—all users of natural family planning—who shared so much with me in private, personal interviews. Another 164 returned detailed six-page essay-type questionnaires telling me about their experiences in this intimate area of their marriage. It is to the openness and generosity of these people that I owe my awareness that natural family planning is a life-style that happens to include highly effective birth control.

PART ONE

❂❂❂❂❂❂❂

Male and
Female Fertility:
A Shared Adventure

1

The Story
Behind This Book

I didn't realize that I had a "way" of thinking about my reproductive power until I met a young attractive psychologist who had been a longtime user of contraception before she learned about natural family planning. I still remember her comments:

> I used to think of my fertility as being something like a slimy green monster lurking in a dark closet, ready to strike with a pregnancy at any time. For years I felt helpless against the "monster" unless I was "armed" with the most powerful contraceptives on the market. What a sad, pathetic view to have held for so many years!

The young woman's description made me aware that human fertility evokes a multiplicity of responses—some of them very strong. While I have never viewed my fertility in such hostile terms—after all, making friendly little babies *is* its sole purpose—certainly there was a time when my reproductive power seemed mysterious, capricious, and highly unpredictable. I did feel that it was "ready to strike with a pregnancy at any time."

Never mind the fact that I knew the textbook details about reproduction. Most of us do. The drawings I saw of the uterus, ovaries, and Fallopian tubes as well as the descriptions of ovulation, conception, and pregnancy bore little relation to day-to-day living. I knew there were days that I couldn't get pregnant, but when *were* they? Lacking this critical information, I had to view my reproductive function as operating willfully, independent of my control.

That thinking seems strange to me today, now that I know the few days that I can get pregnant and all the days that I can't. Learning all of this seemed complicated at first, but I was surprised to realize that after the first three cycles, during which time I paid careful attention to all my fertility signs, I could easily tell the few days when I was fertile.

Thanks to this new awareness, it seems unimaginable to me to rely on interventive technologies, like contraceptive creams, jellies, chemicals, "plugs" of any description, drugs, or barriers. Certainly I will never come face-to-face with a surgeon's tools.

And speaking of surgeon's tools . . .

Not only is fertility awareness a special knowledge that is both comforting and a relief from health anxieties, but it is also knowledge that is *freeing*. I just read, for example, that over a quarter of the married women in the United States have been sterilized. Talk about losing the freedom to choose! And giving it up in the era of increasing options for women!

So I am really grateful for my knowledge of natural family planning, for my fertility awareness. And like many wonderful things that happen to us, I first learned about natural family planning quite by accident. . . .

It was a beautiful spring day back in 1977. I was stuck indoors with work to do but neither interest nor desire to do it. Idly, I picked up a women's magazine that a friend had left behind. As I paged through it, I noticed one of those familiar roundups on birth control that have become regular features. This particular article made passing mention of a natural birth control alternative that was not calendar rhythm. It also reported that a major study evaluating the effectiveness of two major natural methods—again, neither of them rhythm—was under way at Cedars-Sinai Hospital in Los Angeles.

Those two sentences—there were only two—riveted me.

As a medical writer, I knew that the event of ovulation occurs during a very narrow time frame—twenty-four hours or less—and that sperm cells survive less than five days in the woman's reproductive tract. When the sperm's estimated (maximum) survival time of five days is combined with the woman's single day of fertility, then there are less than six days out of every cycle that lovemaking can cause pregnancy. Six days—barely 20 percent of the average cycle—that's all!

Thus, I knew that if there were a reliable, effective means of bracketing the fertile time, we could have a hazard-free, noninterruptive, and, yes, natural method of birth control available. Think of the benefits! It would be possible to plan a family without:

- Resorting to powerful drugs
- Using chemicals
- Wearing interfering barrier devices
- Suffering any side effects whatsoever
- Permanently affecting either spouse's fertility
- Spending money!

Pill Concern: My introduction to natural family planning (NFP) coincided with a Planned Parenthood conference that I attended that fall in Atlanta. I remember how word spread among us very suddenly: A study had just been published in *The Lancet,* a distinguished British medical journal read worldwide, showing that there was a conspicuously higher death rate for women who had ever used the Pill as compared to nonusers. And the sampling was significant: Some 46,000 women of childbearing age in the United Kingdom had been evaluated.

As concern spread like wildfire through the audience (almost none of us had seen the report before the conference), I couldn't help but remember the Pill's 1960 debut and the excitement that surrounded it. And as the years and decades have unfolded, I still find myself contrasting that early excitement with the health concerns about the Pill that have grown unabated year by year. The powerful little tablet has been the subject of claims and counterclaims—many of them very serious—for a long time.

The IUD: But I don't mean to single out the Pill. Let's not forget that the intrauterine device (IUD) also made its bow on the contraceptive scene in the early 1960s. Another "easy" method, it didn't take off like the Pill, but the IUD certainly had its enthusiasts. Today? The attitude toward the contraceptive is, well, cautious.

To be sure, the Dalkon Shield, which was withdrawn from the market, has garnered the heaviest negative headlines—and lawsuits—but all IUD varieties have been linked with health hazards. Problems include the surgical emergency of a perforated uterus and, slightly less serious, the embedding of the device in the uterine wall. But possibly most common of all are the pelvic inflammations and infections which can sometimes impair fertility. Moreover, there is acute concern if a woman develops a pelvic infection *and* becomes accidentally pregnant: "The combination of infection and pregnancy is potentially fatal for an IUD user," report the authors of *Contraceptive Technology,*[1] a well-known, authoritative source for information on artificial birth control.

Sterilization: Considering all the risks of the Pill and the IUD, two noninterruptive birth control methods, it isn't surprising that more and more men and women (but especially women) have opted for surgical sterilization. Over the past decade better procedures have been developed. Still, none, including vasectomy, is 100 percent effective: Pregnancy rates as high as 2 percent have been reported for some of the procedures. Moreover, there are risks, including a mortality rate of 1 to 10 per 100,000 for female sterilizations.

The complication rate varies widely: It is 5 percent for vasectomy, but the female procedures show a range from a low of 1.6 percent to a high of 13.3 percent for culdoscopy.[2] And what could possibly go wrong? Anything from wound infections, uterine perforation, and bladder injuries to bowel burns.

But for most, sterilization does the job . . . with one major drawback: Although there is some limited success in reversing a sterilization, in fact it should be viewed as permanent. It almost always is.

The Contraceptive Future: Over the next several years we will undoubtedly hear more about contraceptive vaccines, improved long-acting IUDs and tailless IUDs, reversible sterilization procedures, a sperm-incapacitating pill for men, and who knows what else? But in contemplating the contraceptive future, it is hard not to look back a scant few decades to consider all the really effective artificial birth control methods that have already been developed. Perhaps you will agree with this observation: As the effectiveness and convenience of interventive birth control methods increase, there seems to be a proportionate increase in the methods' adverse risks and effects.

Take the barrier methods. They're not as effective as the Pill or surgical sterilization, and nobody likes their messiness or inconvenience. But apart from infection problems and allergic reactions for some users and a slight risk of toxic shock syndrome (TSS) associated with diaphragm use, nobody has died from using any of the barriers. And nobody has ever had to surrender his or her fertility for good.

By contrast, the Pill, IUD, and sterilization can be praised for high effectiveness and convenience. The praise is deserved, but the advantages don't come for free. Every user accepts a degree of known risk as well as some unknown risks. Some users surrender their fertility for good in the effectiveness and convenience exchange. Usually the surrender is deliberate (sterilization), but some IUD and Pill users have found themselves infertile for keeps—an effect that was never intended and which can be devastating.

Natural Family Planning: That spring afternoon when I first read about natural family planning, I realized that I was reading about a real newcomer to the birth control scene. What's more, this newcomer depended on a radically different view of human fertility: that it be accepted as a natural and normal condition. We NFP users don't fight our fertility; we live in harmony with it. The reward is *fertility control equivalent to the best interventive methods* (like sterilization and the Pill) but with *no* health risks.

But these advantages don't come for free either. All the new natural birth control methods depend on the day-by-day observation of our bodily fertility signs, which change in response to our condition of fertility or infertility. The three fertility changes that can be monitored are:

- The changes in cervical mucus secretions
- The fluctuations of the basal body temperature
- The alterations of the cervix

When you use NFP to avoid pregnancy, you can have intercourse anytime the signs indicate *infertility*. Then your lovemaking will be able to remain completely free and natural but, of course, you won't conceive.

On the other hand, you may want to get pregnant. No

problem. Just check the body signs and make sure that you have intercourse when they signal *fertility.*

There are important, long-term benefits to learning the fertile signs. You will have a safe method to use during all your major reproductive events, including after childbirth, while breast-feeding, and during that difficult time, the premenopause. And you can use natural family planning even if you have highly irregular, even erratic, cycles.

You certainly wouldn't be able to use calendar rhythm if you were irregular. This is because calendar rhythm presumes that a record of your *past* cycles can be used to predict fertility in your *future* cycles. Obviously, if you are irregular, you will be unable to make any prediction about the length of *any* cycle.

In fact, rhythm presents even greater problems.

Advantages of NFP Over Calendar Rhythm

Every woman is "irregular" at the time of all her major reproductive events—after childbirth, while breast-feeding, and during the premenopause. Thus, calendar rhythm is unreliable for *all* women during *some* of their lives.

By contrast, the new, breakthrough methods of natural family planning represent a radically new approach to a noncontraceptive method of fertility control. You will learn how to observe your fertile signs on a day-to-day basis.

No predictions are involved.

No backward glances to evaluate past cycles are involved.

No rhythm is involved!

The only matter for consideration is the current cycle. More to the point: Each *day* of the current cycle is considered on an individual basis. This means that you will have to ask yourself only one question: Do my body signs *for today* indicate infertility? If they do, you can have intercourse without conceiving a new life. But if the body signs indicate fertility, and you don't want to conceive, just defer relations until your body signs show that you are infertile once again.

By the time my earlier book, *No-Pill, No-Risk Birth Control,* was completed, I had made three separate visits to Cedars-Sinai Hospital in Los Angeles. In addition, I had attended the full course of instruction in natural methods given at Holy Name Hospital in Teaneck, New Jersey, and several classes offered by the Twin Cities Natural Family Planning Center at North Memorial Center in Minneapolis, Minnesota. For several years I attended every International Symposium on Natural Family Planning held at St. John's University in Collegeville, Minnesota. Researchers from all over the world presented papers at those symposia, including:

- Switzerland's Dr. Rudolf F. Vollman, the world's most renowned researcher on the menstrual cycle and former head of the Section on Obstetrics, Perinatal Research Branch, National Institutes of Health, Bethesda, Maryland
- Dr. Robert M. Nakamura, associate professor, Department of Obstetrics and Gynecology at University of Southern California Medical Center in Los Angeles
- Dr. Josef Roetzer, of Voecklabruck, Austria, who has developed the most reliable guidelines that exist today for the use of natural family planning—and whose guidelines I have adapted for this book
- Dr. Edward F. Keefe, a pioneer researcher in the natural methods of birth control and the first person to write about cervical mucus changes and to describe and photograph the cervical changes associated with female fertility

I also read extensively in the literature and, possibly most important of all, I went into the field, so to speak, and interviewed hundreds of men and women who were users of natural family planning. As you will learn, there are psychological ramifications of using a natural birth control method as compared to an artificial one. Personally, I found this area of exploration the most fascinating of all.

New Developments: My earlier book appeared in 1980 and has sold tens of thousands of copies. But during the half decade after its publication, much more was learned about women's fertility. For example, the effects of stress on the fertility signs became better understood. More information about the cervical changes became available, including their usefulness for the woman with a tipped uterus.

Issues about breast-feeding as a means of birth control are now better understood thanks to research efforts from Africa, Scotland, and Australia. This understanding makes it possible for more of us to use this alternative.

There is more: Better ways of making a record of the fertility changes have been developed in U.S. hospital centers. New research on the biophysical properties of cervical mucus has come out of Sweden, deepening our knowledge of this amazing hydrogel so essential to sperm transport through the cervix.

With this wealth of new information and research available, it was time to create *The New No-Pill, No-Risk Birth Control,* the book you are now holding in your hands.

The Effectiveness of NFP: Despite all the new information we have at our fingertips, one matter remains unchanged: natural family planning's high degree of effectiveness. It is not 100 percent—no method, including surgical sterilization, is—but you will be pleased to know that you can expect 99.2 percent reliability if you correctly follow the guidelines in this book. Thus, natural family planning can—and does—match the effectiveness of surgical sterili-zation and the combination Pill.

This high degree of reliability and safety—not to mention the personal control and automony that natural family planning preserves—prompts almost every woman who learns her fertility signs to say, "I wish I had known about this sooner." I certainly said it.

The New No-Pill, No-Risk Birth Control is my contribu-tion to making this information more widely available to all of us.

2

❖❖❖❖❖❖❖

How Male and Female Bodies Cooperate To Conceive a Child

If you viewed sperm cells under magnification, you would note immediately that they resemble tiny tadpoles. Once they are in the female reproductive tract, their tails whip back and forth with astonishing speed, propelling them toward the egg. Upon arrival, the sperm seem to bombard the giant egg, which is 100,000 times larger than the sperm. Each sperm has only one mission: acceptance and entry deep into the egg cell nucleus.

And only one will succeed.

Why is one sperm successful and the others not? We don't know. A mysterious process of selection or attraction seems to be at work and we simply do not understand what it is.

But we do know this: When the nuclei of the sperm cell and the egg cell intereact, something remarkable happens. There comes a moment—after twenty minutes to perhaps an hour or so—when there are no longer two separate entities, a sperm cell and an egg cell. Rather, a unique, single-celled human being exists. Some of the original egg cell matter remains, but the new being has an entirely distinctive structure and identity.

Thus, conception is an example at its most splendid of profound cooperation in nature. Two, male and female, are absolutely essential for the one, male *or* female, to exist.

And as you read further, you will realize that conception is also two things at once: the beginning of a new life, and the culmination of certain physical changes in the male and female bodies that make new life possible.

The Male's Essential Contribution

You may never have thought of it this way, but from the time of puberty until the day he dies, the male is always potentially fertile. Indeed, his reproductive period can stretch for forty, fifty, sixty years, and even longer.

How is it that the male's organs can work so constantly, so continuously? How is it that men are always fertile?

Male Organs: Male external genitals are clearly differentiated and readily visible. They are comprised of the penis and the scrotum, the saclike structure suspended beneath the penis.

You will notice (figure 2.1) that inside the scrotum are two plum-sized structures, the testes, or testicles. One specialized group of cells within the testes produces the masculinizing hormone testosterone. This hormone, which is absorbed directly into a man's bloodstream from the testicular manufacturing site, is responsible for his facial and body (including pubic) hair, voice change, and the awakening of sexual interest.

Sperm Cell Development: Another specialized group of cells within the testes produces immature sperm cells. These cells are located in coiled microscopic tubules, called

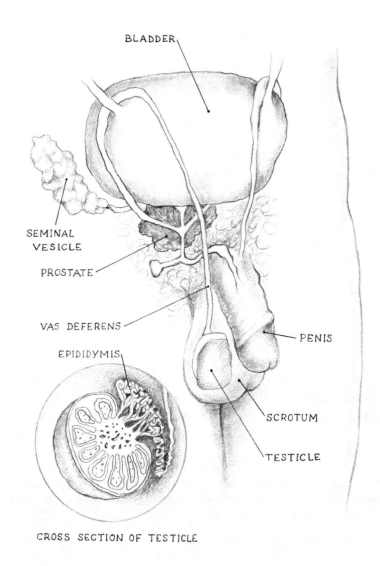

CROSS SECTION OF TESTICLE

Figure 2.1

The Male Reproductive Organs

seminiferous tubules. When sperm cells first leave the germination site, they can't move by themselves. Instead, they are pushed along a special path by contractions of very delicate muscle fibers.

Sperm cells travel very slowly as they are moved into the epididymis, a microscopic tube about twenty feet in length that looks a little like a densely packed spaghetti strand. When sperm cells first enter, they are not capable of fertilization. Then during their slow, two-week passage through the tube they achieve their maximal fertilization capability as well as their famous swimming capability.

If the male remains continent for a long period of time, the sperm cells that have completed their journey are stored at the end of the epididymis near where it joins the vas deferens. These cells don't remain in storage indefinitely; new sperm cells are constantly being produced and mature sperm are removed periodically, even daily.

Assuring Fresh Sperm Supply: One way to rid the body of older sperm is the phenomenon of the involuntary orgasm: the so-called wet dream or nocturnal emission. But even without an involuntary ejaculation, nature has another way of removing aging sperm: leaking them out in the urine. This "leakage" seems to be a continuous process, since sperm are usually found in the urine of normally fertile men.

In most cases (assuming an ongoing genital relationship) most of the sperm leaves the male as a result of the orgasmic involuntary muscle contractions produced during intercourse. At this time the sperm passes through the vas deferens and becomes mixed with other fluids in accessory glands, especially the prostate and seminal vesicles. The term used for the product of this mixture is semen.

Effects of Intercourse: The ejaculation during genital intercourse carries some 200 million sperm from the male tract into the female tract in the seminal fluid. Gradually, over a period of hours, these fluids drain out of the vagina. There is one exception: There is a phase in every woman's cycle during which sperm cells are nourished and kept viable for several days within a woman's reproductive tract. But understanding this survival mechanism requires a consideration of the female reproductive system.

The Female's Essential Contribution

The uterus is flanked on each side by an ovary, which is where all the woman's eggs are stored (figure 2.2). A tube near each ovary is connected to the uterus, which is pear-shaped. The lowest part of the uterus, called the cervix,

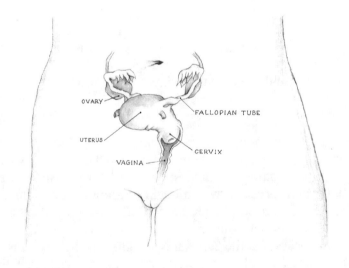

Figure 2.2

The Female Reproductive Organs

protrudes into the vagina. The sperm pass through the cervix and, if conception occurs and there is a normal childbirth, the fetus will pass out of his or her mother's uterus through this opening.

The Menstrual Period: In each menstrual cycle a woman of normal fertility releases one egg (and occasionally more) from either the left or the right ovary. The event is called ovulation.

If conception does not take place, the uterine lining that had been preparing for that possibility—in effect, creating a biological cradle to hold the prenatal child—is sloughed off. This is menstruation.

Menstruation usually occurs between twelve and sixteen days after ovulation, although for a very small percentage of women it can occur in as few as four to nine days after ovulation. In others it may be as long as eighteen, nineteen, twenty days, or more after ovulation. While the time span between ovulation and menstruation is quite constant for most women, the time that elapses from menstruation to menstruation is not. But to understand why, it is essential to understand the events leading to ovulation.

How Ovulation Occurs: A woman's ovaries contain a staggering number of eggs—approximately 400,000. Some 400 times during her lifetime about 1,000 of these eggs will attempt to enter the final stage of maturity. But the egg maturation process, which occurs during every cycle, is a little like a footrace: There may be a thousand entrants, but there is only one winner.

It appears that the egg that is ovulated in each cycle is the one that takes the developmental lead in that "cast of a thousand." For some reason, once a particular egg cell gets its head start, it seems never to lose its front position. Soon, all the other eggs competing for development will degenerate and die.

Ovulation itself is triggered by an internal "fertility trigger" found in the tiny pituitary gland. The pituitary, which is located in the base of the brain, emits special hormones, one of which stimulates the growth and development of the ovarian follicles containing the eggs. It is called the follicle-stimulating hormone—FSH for short.

Curiously, the length of time it takes for FSH to initiate the active ripening of the follicles, and therefore the eggs, can be highly variable and unpredictable, unlike the unvarying two-week postovulatory predictability of menstruation. The ripening process can take a week; *it can also take months*. But once the amount of FSH released into the body reaches a special "threshold" level, things move quickly *and predictably*.

Within five days a special group of ovarian follicles that contain eggs are stimulated into active maturation. One of the marks of this stimulation is the secretion of estradiol, the major estrogenic hormone that enters the bloodstream from the follicle and travels up to the pituitary. Its appearance is a signal to the pituitary that the follicles are stimulated.

Once this signal is received, the gland immediately cuts back on FSH production so that no competing follicles can ripen. Then it sends out a different hormone, the luteinizing hormone (LH). This hormone boosts a single follicle into the final stage that culminates in its rupture so that one egg cell can be released.

Occasionally more than one follicle achieves the final stage, with the result that two or more eggs are ovulated. When this happens, a woman conceives nonidentical twins.

Once the egg (or eggs) finally erupts from the ovary, tiny miscroscopic hairs lining the fimbriae, the tentaclelike structures making up the "trumpet" ends of the Fallopian tubes, instantly grasp the egg and whisk it into the interior. The whole process takes less than twenty seconds, from the moment the egg cell is released from the ovary until it is tucked safely within the Fallopian tube.

Perfect Timing: Here is the fascinating part: It is only in the last few hours before the follicle ruptures that the major events of maturation occur for the egg, according to Thomas W. Hilgers, M.D., assistant professor of obstetrics and gynecology at Creighton University School of Medicine in Omaha, Nebraska. Consequently, it is irrelevant how long any particular cycle lasts. In fact, all estimated 400,000 eggs in the woman's ovaries are present *before* she is born, from about the tenth week of her fetal development. *The essential matter is proper maturation.* Since this takes place only after FSH production has been cut and LH has entered the bloodstream, and within a very short but well-defined time period, the egg that is ovulated emerges at the peak of its development—when it is ripe for conception.

Thus, nature has designed multiple stratagems to ensure that both sperm cells and egg cells emerge at the perfect time—at their peaks—to maximize the possibility of conception. But as you will learn in the next few pages, there is considerably more involved in a successful conception than the mere production of fresh egg cells and sperm cells.

How Conception Occurs

In the first few hours after ovulation, the egg is held in the Fallopian tube, about halfway toward the uterus. After an ejaculation that takes place during intercourse, the sperm travel upward from the vaginal canal, through the cervix and the uterus and into the Fallopian tubes. It is there, in one of the Fallopian tubes, that the egg may join with one of the male cells to create a new individual. But if no sperm are present or if no conception takes place, the egg disintegrates.

Egg disintegration usually ends within twenty-four hours after ovulation. Some authorities believe that it ends within eight hours. In any case, whether the time frame is less than

twenty-four hours or less than eight hours, *a woman is capable of becoming pregnant only within twenty-four hours of the day she ovulates—not later, not before.*

Achieving Conception: This brings us to another question: If the egg survives less than twenty-four hours out of each cycle, how is it possible to become pregnant more easily than not? How likely is it to time intercourse precisely for pregnancy to occur?

To be sure, some mammals—rabbits and ferrets are two examples—ovulate in response to copulation, but this is *not* the human pattern. Instead, nature has a way of "stretching out" a woman's fertile phase: Sperm are kept alive for a number of days in the female tract, but *only* during the time in her cycle when the woman is about to ovulate. In this way, fewer acts of intercourse are as likely to lead to conception as numerous acts.

Indeed, this is one of nature's most fascinating stratagems to ensure that the human species survives. It lies at the cornerstone of all modern, scientific natural family planning methods. But how exactly does it work? What is its mechanism?

Vaginal Secretions: Most of the time a woman's vaginal secretions are acidic and actively hostile to sperm. This ensures against the possibility of sperm living—and aging— in the woman's reproductive tract. But if any sperm are particularly plucky and withstand the acid environment, nature provides a second, more effect mechanism to ensure that sperm won't travel beyond the vaginal canal: the mucus barrier.

Early Mucus: Three types of cervical mucus have been identified. The early mucus, so-called G-mucus, shows a dense maze of tight-knit, meshlike formations when

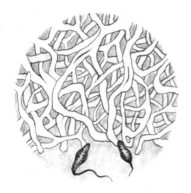

examined under an electron microscope. The cervix is "plugged" with this type of mucus prior to ovulation and soon after. Early mucus is an effective barrier to sperm because the little male cells simply cannot penetrate this maze. But matters change considerably as the time of ovulation approaches.

Figure 2.3
Early mucus is a barrier to sperm.

Developing Mucus: About five days prior to ovulation, the little mucus strands cease to "crosshatch" against each other so completely. As a result, possible travel routes for the sperm cells open up. The structure of the second mucus type, L-mucus, is still dense, but sperm cells can at least manage to penetrate it, although they are slowed considerably in their travel.

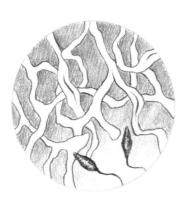

Figure 2.4
Developing mucus can be penetrated by sperm cells.

Peak Mucus: Finally, the mucus strands arrange themselves in a parallel-type formation, becoming, in effect, a gateway—forming an "entry-type" mucus, known as S-mucus, that does more than just ease sperm penetration. *Entry-type mucus actively enhances sperm cell penetration through the cervix.*

Figure 2.5
Peak mucus enhances
sperm cell penetration.

Biological Valve: This dramatic change in the mucus is a result of hormone activity. As follicular activity enters its final stages before ovulation, increasing amounts of estrogen are secreted. Estrogen acts on cervical mucus, changing it from a thick, tenacious gummy mass, hostile to sperm (G-mucus), to a thin, creamy intermediate substance (L-mucus) that allows some sperm penetration, before becoming an abundant, clear, watery solution that looks and feels like raw egg white (S-mucus) and is highly favorable to sperm cell penetration. Estrogen is responsible for "lifting the barriers" and making the mucus an effective, watery medium for sperm migration just prior to ovulation—the optimal time for conception to occur.

It is in this fashion that a woman's cervical mucus secretions act like a biological valve, a valve that opens and closes in exquisite harmony with each woman's ovulation pattern. As a result, when sperm are splashed against entry-type mucus at the cervical opening, a few will actually be able to penetrate through the cervix. This is because it is near the time that an egg will be released from the ovary.

The few sperm cells that first penetrate through the mucus will quickly be followed by additional male cells. The sperm actually appear to follow one another like a column of army ants on the march. The sperm are swimming toward the possible site of conception: the Fallopian tubes.

Sperm can make the trip to the Fallopian tubes in less than an hour. The male cells enter both tubes even though only one of the tubes holds an egg in each cycle. The sperm continue traveling straight through the tubes until they eventually tumble out into the abdominal cavity. Of course, there is one exception: that special sperm that actually penetrates the egg cell and succeeds in causing a conception.

Sperm Cell Storage: Of course, pregnancy would be unlikely if intercourse took place a day or so before ovulation and all the sperm had already sailed through—and out—of the Fallopian tubes. Thus, nature has devised an "insurance" mechanism: the cervical crypts. There are about a hundred of them located along the inside wall of the cervix (figure 2.6).

Most of the sperm cells in each ejaculation are led into these tiny cavities. The crypts act like holding areas, storing sperm cells and keeping them nourished and alive. The storage is temporary, however: Sperm are continuously released from the crypts over a period of days. This "gradual release" is nature's special mechanism to ensure that healthy male cells will be in the vicinity of the egg during that critical—and brief—six-to-eight-hour period after it is ovulated.

One in Several Hundred Million: Now perhaps you can begin to understand more completely what a remarkable

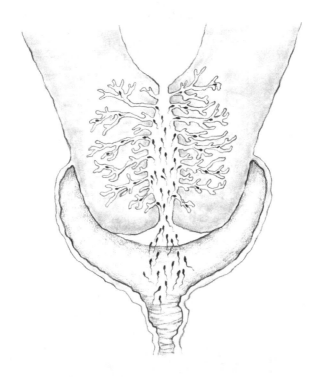

Figure 2.6
The cervical crypts act as "holding" areas for sperm cells, keeping
them nourished and alive for up to five days.

event your conception was. Nature carefully designed an
array of special biological mechanisms to ensure that an egg
cell and a sperm cell would be likely to join and interact
when both were at their peak.

In your case, for example, only *that* special sperm cell
and *that* special egg cell from your parents could have
created you. And if you think of the number of sperm cells

at each ejaculation (several hundred million) and the number of egg cells available for ripening at each ovulation (up to several hundred thousand), you can see why it can truly be said that *you are one in trillions!*

And the same can be said for every child you conceive.

3

✿✝✿✝✿✝✿✝✿

How Your Body Tells You That You Are Ready to Conceive a Child

While a normal, healthy man is fertile every hour of his life from puberty to death, this splendid day-in, day-out, year-in, year-out fertility is completely useless without a woman. Even if a man were to have intercourse with a female of normal fertility, conception is still not assured, since most of the time a woman is infertile.

Thus, male production of several million and more sperm cells is absolutely worthless in the absence of a woman's single, critical contribution: one viable egg cell. And at a certain point, within twenty-four hours after a woman has ovulated, a couple *cannot conceive again under any circumstances whatsoever until the beginning of the fertile phase of her next menstrual cycle.*

Then, once the fertile phase has begun, intercourse can lead to conception, the likelihood increasing as the woman nears the time of ovulation. Indeed, even male-female genital contact *without* penile entry into the vagina or without ejaculation can lead to conception. The reason? If the woman is in the fertile phase of her cycle, there may be

27

TABLE 1

MENSTRUAL/POSTMENSTRUAL PHASE	OVULATORY PHASE	POSTOVULATORY PHASE
Couple is infertile	Couple is fertile / Conception is likely	Couple is infertile

Menstrual/Postmenstrual Phase	Ovulatory Phase	Postovulatory Phase
1 2 3 4 5 6 7 8 9 10 11 12 13 14 15 16 17 18 19 20 21 22 23	24 25 26 27 28 29 30 31 32 33	34 35 36 37 38 39 40 41 42 43 44
1 2 3 4 5 6 7 8 9 10 11 12	13 14 15 16 17 18 19 20 21 22	23 24 25 26 27 28 29 30 31 32 33
1 2 3 4 5 6 7 8 9 10 11 12 13 14 15	16 17 18 19 20 21 22 23 24 25	26 27 28 29 30 31 32 33 34 35 36
1 2 3 4 5 6 7 8 9 10 11 12 13 14 15 16 17	18 19 20 21 22 23 24 25 26 27	28 29 30 31 32 33 34 35 36 37 38
1 2 3 4 5	6 7 8 9 10 11 12 13 14 15	16 17 18 19 20 21 22 23 24 25 26
1 2 3 4 5 6 7 8 9 10 11 12 13 14 15 16 17 18 19 20 21 22	23 24 25 26 27 28 29 30 31 32	33 34 35 36 37 38 39 40 41 42 43
1 2 3 4 5 6	7 8 9 10 11 12 13 14 15 16	17 18 19 20 21 22 23 24 25 26 27
1 2 3 4 5 6 7 8	9 10 11 12 13 14 15 16 17 18	19 20 21 22 23 24 25 26 27 28 29
1 2 3 4 5 6 7 8 9 10 11 12 13 14	15 16 17 18 19 20 21 22 23 24	25 26 27 28 29 30 31 32 33 34 35
1 2 3 4 5 6 7 8 9	10 11 12 13 14 15 16 17 18 19	20 21 22 23 24 25 26 27 28 29 30
1 2 3 4 5 6 7 8 9 10 11 12 13	14 15 16 17 18 19 20 21 22 23	24 25 26 27 28 29 30 31 32 33 34
1 2 3 4 5 6 7 8 9 10 11 12 13 14 15 16	17 18 19 20 21 22 23 24 25 26	27 28 29 30 31 32 33 34 35 36 37

The length of the menstrual/postmenstrual phase is highly variable for different women and can even vary from cycle to cycle for the same woman. It is the variability in this phase that determines the total length of each cycle; the lengths of the ovulatory and postovulatory phases remain highly constant for all women.

enough sperm in the preejaculatory fluids that come into contact with the appropriate secretions on her vulva to result in pregnancy.

Obviously, the changes in a woman's body are the critical ones to recognize in avoiding pregnancy. This is why you need detailed information on the signs indicating fertility and infertility. By recognizing these signs, you can know on a *day-to-day* basis whether or not intercourse is likely to cause conception.

This knowledge gives you special power. Your "fertility awareness" can be used however you mutually agree to use it: either to postpone or avoid conception, or to welcome a child into your lives.

It is your choice.

Postovulatory Infertility

Table 1 shows twelve different menstrual cycles from twelve different women. The first day of menstruation is day 1 of a new cycle.

You will notice that the length of the ovulatory and postovulatory phases is constant for all twelve women. This is because no matter how long a woman's cycle is—and these cycles range from 26 to 44 days—the ovulatory and postovulatory phases remain constant, since menstruation generally occurs about 12 to 16 days after ovulation.

In contrast, the menstrual/postmenstrual phase is *highly variable* for different women, and it can also vary a few days from cycle to cycle for the same woman. It is the variability in *this* phase that determines the total length of each of your cycles.

While we usually think of the menstrual/postmenstrual phase as the beginning of a new cycle, it is also a *continuation* of the postovulatory phase. You can see this quite readily by looking at table 2, on page 30, where the cycle is drawn as a circle. Note that a couple's infertility is continu-

TABLE 2

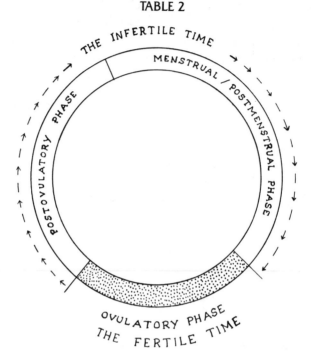

Infertility is continuous from the beginning of the postovulatory phase through the end of the menstrual/postmenstrual phase.

ous through the postovulatory and the menstrual/postmenstrual phases.

It is important to note this continuous phase of infertility because study after study has shown that there is absolutely no chance for conception once a woman has entered the postovulatory phase of her cycle.[1] Conception becomes likely only when she enters the ovulatory phase of the *succeeding* cycle, when the cervical mucus secretions change into a solution that not only is hospitable to sperm but actually aids their survival.

Determining the Infertile Time: One method gives you the highest possible assurance that the postovulatory infertile phase has begun. Thus, it offers you reliability equivalent to the Pill or tubal sterilization. What is involved? Only this: monitoring your basal body temperature every morning. Every woman's waking temperatures change throughout her cycle. They are lower at the beginning of the cycle; they are about a half a degree higher during the last two weeks. *When a woman's waking temperatures have reached a sustained high level, she is infertile.* Pregnancy cannot take place once a woman has entered the high temperature phase of the cycle.

Explaining Your Temperature Rise: Why does your temperature rise in the final two weeks of your cycle? What causes it?

Here is what happens: After the egg cell is released, the ovarian follicle that originally contained it begins to manufacture the hormone *progesterone*. Progesterone does three things:

1. Causes a woman's basal body temperature to rise,
2. Dries up cervical mucus, and
3. Suppresses all further ovulations for the rest of the cycle.*

But please recognize that you *cannot* pinpoint the day of ovulation from a review of your temperatures. *The only*

---

*Progesterone has another essential task if conception takes place: It helps prepare the uterine lining for the implantation of a tiny embryo. If conception has occurred in that particular cycle, the follicle will continue to produce progesterone to sustain the pregnancy.

In fact, one way of discovering if you are pregnant even before the doctor can tell is to note whether the high level of progesterone is sustained in your body for seven days beyond the expected beginning of the menstrual period. So if your waking temperature remains elevated for a full week beyond its usual elevated duration, you have 99 percent assurance that pregnancy has been achieved.

*thing temperatures can tell you is when your infertile time
has definitely begun.* Acts of intercourse that take place
during the infertile phase cannot result in conception.

Don't worry about how to apply this information at this
point. Right now, I just want to give you a detailed overview of the signs. Soon enough, in part 2 of this book, you
will receive specific instructions on charting your temperatures and all the fertility signs.

Research Results: Just how reliable is the so-called temperature method? One study by Dr. Gerhard Doering (West
Germany) followed 307 couples over 11,352 cycles, an
average of almost three years' participation per couple.
There was a total of eight unplanned pregnancies, *not one
of which occurred after a third high temperature had been
properly recorded.* Thus, Doering's study showed 100 percent reliability for the method when intercourse takes place
after the third high temperature is recorded.[2]

Dr. John Marshall, a participant in the June 1966 Geneva
scientific group meeting on the biology of fertility control
by periodic abstinence, has also done work on postovulatory infertility. He reports that in his study in England of
5,013 cycles in which the dates of intercourse were known,
"there was not a single instance of conception occurring
when intercourse had been confined to the phase after three
temperatures at the higher level had been recorded."[3]

Dr. Rudolf F. Vollman followed 74 couples who already
had children (and thus could be presumed to be normally
fertile) and who now wished to have another baby. For
purposes of his study, Dr. Vollman asked the couples to
maintain a record of the wife's waking temperatures and to
have only *one* act of intercourse in the cycle in which they
were hoping to conceive. It was predictable: Not a single
conception occurred to couples whose intercourse took
place after the second day of the temperature rise.[4]

Perhaps you can understand why the well-known population and family planning expert associated with the Population Council, the late Christopher Tietze, M.D., has ranked this natural method with the combination Pill and surgical sterilization as one of the most reliable birth control measures of all.[5] It outranks both the mini-Pill and the IUD in effectiveness.

Although Dr. Tietze didn't mention the fact, I will: This effectiveness is possible *without a single hazard to your health or your fertility.*

Menstrual/Postmenstrual Infertility

Since you cannot conceive after an indisputable temperature rise has been established, all the days between confirmation of the rise and the beginning of the following menstruation (menses) are absolutely infertile. Indeed, if you look back at Table 2, you will note the continuation of infertility through the beginning of the menstrual phase. During this time of infertility, it is impossible to conceive. Thus, intercourse can take place anytime without causing conception.

But there is a new question: How long does infertility last in the menstrual/postmenstrual phase? How long can you have relations without conception taking place?

Continuation of Infertility: You remain infertile during the menstrual/postmenstrual phase for an indeterminate length of time. The single most important fertility indicator is the development and change in your cervical mucus secretions, something you can easily learn to monitor once you know what to look for.

What to Look For: The changes in mucus have been recognized since the late 1930s and early 1940s by physicians working with infertile couples. In the 1960s two Australian physicians—a husband and wife, Drs. John and Evelyn Billings—realized that women could learn to monitor the changes in their mucus secretions just from observation of the vulva, the external female genital area.

The mucus changes follow one another in a regular, *unfolding* pattern and do *not* depend on cyclic regularity. You will observe these changes whether your cycles are long or short. The only difference is that beginning mucus changes may be delayed or intermittent, ultimately determining the "cycle length."

Once you become alert to the changes—and their meaning in terms of fertility—you will know whether a specific act of intercourse can lead to conception in a new menstrual cycle.

What should you be looking for?

The Infertile Preovulatory Phase

Let us assume that your menstrual bleeding ended after about four or five days. The vagina itself will be moist, but externally there is a distinct sensation of dryness. You may even notice a feeling of mild itchiness around the vaginal entrance. Perhaps a little additional estrogen is entering your system, but at this point there is not enough to create any real changes in the cervical mucus—at least, not any changes you can detect. Thus, there will usually be a handful of so-called dry days.

You are infertile during the dry days. Acts of intercourse will not lead to conception when the vagina is without mucus.

The Fertile Ovulatory Phase

Assuming you don't have short cycles in which the ovulatory phase immediately follows the menstrual bleeding, you will notice mucus for the first time sometime after the dry days have passed. The onset of mucus marks the possible beginning of the ovulatory phase.

Early Mucus: The first mucus you see will probably be of a special consistency. Perhaps the best way to explain it is to remind you of school days when you sometimes used a white paste that was sticky and tacky. The first mucus you observe (so-called G-mucus) may remind you of that paste.

You won't have to go searching for the mucus, since it is usually readily detectable near the vaginal opening. Sticky, tacky mucus is usually opaque white or yellow. It is also rather thick and will hold its shape very well, making tiny peaks when you place it between the fingers and then separate them (figure 3.1).

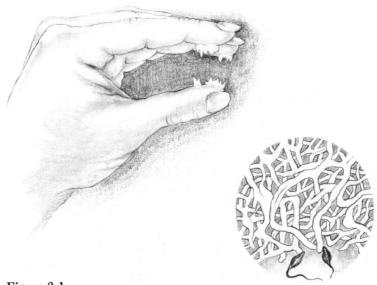

Figure 3.1

Early mucus is sticky, tacky, and opaque in color.

Microscopically and chemically, the sticky, tacky mucus is still a barrier to sperm. However, the secretions can change over a period of hours (in less than a half day or so) into developing mucus, which is *not* a barrier to sperm.

Developing Mucus: When the cervical secretions become thin, watery, possibly milky, and rather cloudy-looking—like smooth, creamy hand lotion—your body may be preparing for ovulation. You could definitely conceive a child!

The thin, watery, or cloudy mucus (so-called L-mucus) is detectable on the external genitals just by a feeling of wetness that was previously absent. In addition, you will notice that if you get a dab of mucus between two fingers and draw them apart, it won't make little peaks; it will either remain smooth on both fingers, like a dab of creamy hand lotion, or stretch up to a quarter of an inch between the fingers (figure 3.2).

This type of mucus may also look somewhat translucent, whether it is yellow or white in color. You may sometimes notice that it appears to be a little bit red, pink, or brown. This is caused by spotting and is perfectly normal for many women. As long as the spotting or bleeding is accompanied by developing mucus, it should not concern you.

The duration of this type of mucus is highly variable for each woman. It could last a day or two or several days.

Occasionally, the mucus reverts to the sticky, tacky consistency for a day or more. However, this change does not alter the fact that your body is in a phase that could result in conception. *You are fertile; acts of intercourse will probably cause pregnancy.*

Peak Mucus: When estrogen is highest in your bloodstream (and there is no progesterone to speak of circulating in your system yet), your mucus will change to look like raw egg white or like the mucus that runs from your nose at the start of a cold—completely clear and "glary" (shiny).

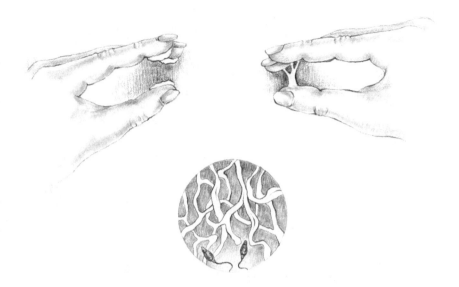

Figure 3.2

Developing mucus, which is thin, watery, or cloudy, is usually detectable on the external genitals. It is a sign of fertility during the pre-ovulatory phase.

The mucus (so-called S-mucus) tends to become profuse at this time. Some women even find it necessary to wear a sanitary napkin. (Figure 3.3)

As for feel and quality, the mucus is much like raw egg white or nasal mucus. If you take a small amount of this mucus between two fingers, it will feel slippery. Then if you draw the fingers apart, the mucus will stretch at least an inch—or even several inches, to a possible ten-inch maximum—until it looks like a long, thin, shimmering thread. The ability of the mucus to be stretched into a thread is an important phenomenon with a special German name: *Spinnbarkeit*.

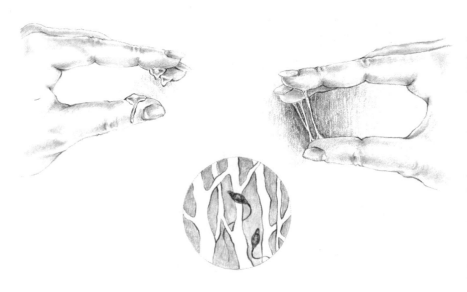

Figure 3.3

Peak mucus feels slippery on the external genitals and can be stretched up to ten inches between the fingers. You are fertile!

You are most likely to conceive during the days when slippery, lubricative mucus is present. Channels are opened wide to enhance sperm travel through the mucus. Do *not* engage in acts of intercourse or genital contact (that is, penis-to-vulva touching or contact without penetration) if you do not wish to conceive a child at this time.

The very last day of the slippery, lubricative mucus is known as the *mucus peak.*

Does the mucus peak mean that your fertile phase is nearly over? Will you be able to consider yourself infertile the next day or two?

No, you won't.

You see, at this stage in our knowledge it is not possible to pinpoint the exact moment of ovulation. However, special hormonal measurements indicate that ovulation can sometimes occur as late as three whole days *after* the mucus peak. It may also occur as early as two days before the peak. However, it is impossible to determine the moment of ovulation, even in the laboratory. For this reason, *our major concern is to "bracket" the fertile days.* This bracketing can be readily accomplished. Certainty about the precise time of ovulation cannot.

So the question comes back to this one: When are you infertile again? When can intercourse take place without conception?

Drying-Up Days: After the mucus peak has passed, a number of dry or drying-up days will usually begin. This is the direct effect of the progesterone's action on the cervical mucus secretions. The estrogen levels may actually be *higher* after ovulation, but they will be *opposed* by the progesterone. The hormone will suppress further ovulations, and at the same time it will cause the mucus to change.

Mucus and Temperature Signs: How do these two signs relate? Shouldn't the drying up coincide with the temperature rise?

Perhaps it should . . . in *theory*. In reality, however, we are not programmed machines.

"If you have seen or felt lots of slippery, lubricative, raw-egg-white mucus in the past two days, continue to abstain no matter what the temperature chart shows," reports Edward F. Keefe, M.D., a pioneer in the development of NFP. "In order words, don't go by temperature in the face of contradictory mucus signs, nor by mucus in the face of sure low-temperature readings."

Indeed, there is no *fixed* time relationship between the mucus peak and ovulation; variation of several days either way is within the range of normalcy, and guidelines have been devised to take these variations into account.

Dr. Josef Roetzer has devised what is probably the easiest and most reliable mucus-with-temperature guidelines: *After the cessation of the fertile-time mucus, look for three consecutive high temperatures above the highest of six consecutive temperatures just before the rise begins. The last of the three temperatures must be at least 0.4° higher than the highest of those six lower temperatures.*

In other words, *after* the mucus peak, when the drying up begins—and *only* after it begins—should you rely on the third of the high temperatures as a confirmation of infertility. Sometimes you may notice one or more days of mucus well after the peak, even after the third high temperature has been recorded. This is a transitory phenomenon. It sometimes occurs, but you can consider yourself infertile provided you followed the guidelines.

Infertility in the New Cycle: Through 1977 Dr. Roetzer had seen no pregnancies from an act of intercourse on day 5 of a new cycle *following a sustained temperature rise in the previous cycle.*[6]

One client in a study of 200 women with over 6,000 doctor-supervised cycles became pregnant from day 6 intercourse. The woman had a history of short (22-to-27-day) cycles and for the previous seven years had had relations through the first 5 days of her new cycle without ever having conceived. "Theoretically," reported Dr. Roetzer at that time, "it seems almost impossible that an intercourse on the sixth day of a genuine cycle should result in a conception."[7] Taking into account the woman's pregnancy, Dr. Roetzer calculated the reliability factor for day 6 infertility in his study to be 99.8 percent, an overall figure for all couples with all kinds of cycle lengths.

In the intervening years there have been other reports of pregnancies resulting from a day 6 intercourse. For example, sperm deposited in the vagina on day 6 survived and caused a conception several days later when ovulation occurred.[8]

In the face of these small numbers of pregnancies, Dr. Roetzer has concluded that there is a small possibility that a woman whose cycles range between 23 and 25 days could be fertile on day 6 in her new cycle, although without broader controlled studies it is impossible to offer an effectiveness figure. So for reliability that will bring you within the range of surgical sterilization on the early days of your cycle, you can go by this guideline:

Very Early Days Guideline

- If your cycles range between 23 and 25 days, consider day 6 to be your *first* fertile day.
- If you *ever* have a cycle of 22 days or less, consider *day 1* to be your first fertile day.

Note: To maintain the highest degree of reliability, I will assume infertility through day 5 only after a sustained temperature rise in the previous cycle. You may decide to use a later cutoff as follows:

Dr. Roetzer has no statistics for the fertility of day 7 per se, but he reports that it can be fertile for some couples, particularly for those who ever experience cycles 27 days or shorter. *By day 7 you should be very alert to possible mucus.*

Day 8 is definitely in the fertile range for couples who experience cycle lengths of at least 28 days.

Effectiveness: Are Dr. Roetzer's guidelines reliable? Can you count on high effectiveness in avoiding pregnancy?

You can.

In a study conducted by Dr. Roetzer, 491 couples of previously proven fertility followed all guidelines over 17,026 cycles, which works out to an average of about three years' participation per couple. In those three years there was a total of only twelve unplanned pregnancies.[9]

Those twelve pregnancies result in a method-effectiveness rate (which is easier to deal with for comparative purposes) of 99.2 percent.

This is also a method that is 100 percent free of any risk to your health or future fertility.

Movement of the Cervix

"Wanted: An Easily Detected Sign of Impending or Just Completed Ovulation." That isn't my snappy title. Dr. Carl G. Hartman, an early pioneer in natural birth control methods, used the title on one of his last papers, published in 1965.

Dr. Hartman's title reflects the yearning of researchers who had long hoped to develop a simple, easy-to-use biological test system to let a woman know when ovulation is about about to occur or is actually occurring. But as often happens in our attempts to outwit nature, nature beat us. As it turns out, every woman carries her own built-in biological test system: her cervix.

Any woman can feel the cervix, the lower part of the uterus, simply by inserting a finger up into the vagina. This part of a woman's internal organs is round, with a small opening in the middle, like a dimple (figure 2.2).

The sperm pass up into the uterus through this opening during the ovulatory phase. If no sperm have passed—or if sperm have passed but conception doesn't take place— then the menstrual bleeding will leave the uterus through the cervix and pass out of the body through the vagina.

Fertility Indicator: Because the cervix changes depending upon a woman's condition of fertility or infertility, many women find it to be a significant factor in helping them develop their fertility awareness. Dr. Edward F. Keefe, the first doctor to have systematically studied and published papers about the changes in the cervix during the ovulatory phase, candidly admits that he first learned about the phenomenon from his patients. He instructed them to probe as high as the cervix if they had difficulty detecting mucus. They had no difficulty doing so, except as the time of ovulation approached when woman after woman reported having difficulty reaching the cervix. Yet when the women were infertile once again, there seemed to be no problem at all. When Dr. Keefe heard this reaction from enough women, he recognized that the condition of the cervix itself could be a significant factor in determining fertility. Keefe launched the first research ever conducted on the cervix as a sign of fertility.

Cervical Changes: There are three changes that occur in the cervix as you move through your cycle: a change in position; a change in the cervical opening (the os); and a change in the texture.

Position Change: As more and more estrogen enters your bloodstream in the preovulatory phase, the estrogens tend to cause a contraction of certain muscles. Result? Over a period of days it will become harder and harder for you to touch your cervix with your fingertip, since it is being progressively drawn *up* into your vagina as much as an inch or more as the muscle contracts. It may even become impossible to touch your cervix, because it has risen so high. (The illustrations in chapter 8 will give you an idea of how your cervix moves up in the vagina as you enter your fertile phase.)

Once your progesterone levels begin to rise, the cervix progressively lowers into the vagina and becomes firm to the touch within days.

Cervical Opening Change: The cervical opening, known as the *os* (Latin for "mouth"), really *opens* at the time of ovulation. If you have had a child and delivered vaginally, the os will look more like a slit and it may even be possible for you to introduce a fingertip into the cervical opening at the time of your fertile peak (see figure 8.4 in chapter 8). During the infertile phase, when there is a high level of progesterone in your system, the os is closed tightly and is sometimes "plugged" with the sticky, tacky mucus that makes the passage resolutely impenetrable to sperm.

Texture Change: The cervix will change from being firm, like the tip of your nose, to being soft, spongy, and sometimes rubbery. It will feel yielding and soft, like your lips. Again, these changes parallel the hormonal fluctuation in the body. When there is more progesterone, the cervix is firm. But as more estrogen enters the bloodstream, the cervix softens and loses its firmness completely. And that, of course, is the time when you are getting close to, or are actually at, the day of ovulation.

Aid to Fertility Awareness: The cervical changes can be very helpful if you are confused about the mucus sign, since it allows you to check one sign against another. You will usually find coincidence between the mucus changes and the cervical movement if you are ovulating normally.

Dr. Keefe has found that about 25 percent of those he has worked with have ranked the cervical changes as being among the most important, easily detectable signs of ovulation. This group used it readily to decide about fertility or infertility in a particular day.

On the other hand, another 25 percent found the cervical

sign to be less valuable than the other fertility indicators. They tended to depend on other signs, even though they were aware of the "biological test system" they carried around in their bodies day in and day out.[10]

Learning to Recognize the Changes: Still, of all the signs of fertility, cervical change is one of the hardest to recognize, especially in the beginning when it is most subjective. "I couldn't figure it out at first," said one woman. "Was the cervix higher? Was it softer? I just wasn't sure. It took me three months before I got the hang of it."

She is like most of us.

In a special survey conducted among 152 Couple to Couple League teachers and candidate teachers, a sizable majority of women (82 percent) needed anywhere from two to six complete cycles of experience before they could reliably detect the cervical changes. A small number (5 percent) needed as long as a year to feel confident in their discernment of the changes, while 3 percent were still not confident about interpreting the cervical changes. (Five percent learned the sign in one cycle; the rest of the respondents left the question unanswered.)[11]

Another interesting finding: While many women readily detect two out of three of the changes (but not all three), a majority of the survey repondents (65 percent) could detect all three changes in their cervices. But in a ranking of three different changes, 75 percent chose the opening and closing of the cervical os as either their first or second most positive sign.

Retroverted Uterus: Women with retroverted (so-called tipped) uteri had no difficulty in using the cervical sign. (A tipped uterus tends to fold backward toward the tailbone rather than slightly forward, toward the front of the pelvis.)

Twenty-five percent of the study respondents had tipped uteri, but none had difficulty in learning and applying the cervical sign. One of the women even had a prolapsed uterus (which means that it sags low in the vagina) but was still able to make the cervical observations.

Other Fertility Indicators

The mucus changes, cervical changes, and temperature shift are all standard fertility/infertility indicators for women. The summary chart on page 47 gives you an at-a-glance overview of the changes.

Besides the three major fertility signs, there are signs experienced by different women which are uniquely their own. For example, some women experience breast tenderness around the time of ovulation. Others feel mild discomfort, even pain, around the time they ovulate. Indeed, for some women, the pain can be quite incapacitating, interfering with their normal duties.

Sometimes the pain is so distinct that a woman is convinced that she can tell which ovary—left or right—is releasing the egg. But note well: *The pain itself cannot be used to pinpoint the day of ovulation.*

Suzanne Parenteau-Carreau, M.D., reports that examinations of ovaries during surgical operations which followed abdominal pain revealed either follicles which were ready to release their eggs or empty follicles which had already extruded their eggs. Dr. Parenteau-Carreau notes: "The fact that [the pain] may be confused with a digestive tract pain or other pain constitutes another limit to this symptom, whose only value ultimately is to confirm more objective signs."[12]

I emphasize this point because I want to keep one matter in the forefront of your mind: Natural methods do not give you any information whatsoever about the *day* of ovulation. The signs of fertility only help you to *bracket* your fertile days. Ovulation pain *can* be used as another indica-

Three Major Signs of Fertility and Infertility

Menstrual/Postmenstrual Phase: *Woman is infertile. Acts of intercourse will not cause pregnancy.*
   Temperature: Low
   Mucus: Dry days (no fertile-time mucus)
   Cervix: Closed, low, and firm
   Duration of phase: Highly variable, lasting from days to many weeks, even several months

Ovulatory Phase: *Woman is fertile; conception is likely. If pregnancy is not desired, avoid intercourse and genital-genital contact.*
   Temperature: Rising
   Mucus: Sticky, tacky mucus developing into fertile-time (slippery, lubricative) mucus, then reverting back to sticky, tacky mucus and/or disappearing
   Cervix: Open, high, and soft
   Duration of phase: Somewhat variable, but usually lasts about seven to eleven days. Still, this phase may last longer in some cases.

Postovulatory Phase: *Woman is infertile. Acts of intercourse will not result in pregnancy.*
   Temperature: High
   Mucus: No fertile-time mucus; occasionally sticky, tacky mucus; usually no mucus ("dry")
   Cervix: Closed, low, and firm
   Duration of phase: Least variable phase of the cycle. It usually lasts about ten to fifteen days for 90 percent of all women.

tor that you are in your fertile phase, but it is *not* proof of ovulation.

I have detailed the three major signs of fertility. In addition, the following is a listing of ovulatory signs that have been reported by some women who use them as additional "bracketing" information. Perhaps you share one or two:

- Bloating (shoes feel tight; rings don't fit)
- Insomnia
- Acne
- Chills
- Cold hands and feet
- Mood changes (depression-to-exuberance swings)
- Gum bleeding
- Greasy hair
- Spotting
- Heavy feeling or dull ache low in the pelvic area at the level of the vulva

Men sometimes report that they can detect the fertile time by changes in the wife's mood and/or by certain physical changes in her body. These are some of the female bodily changes that have been noted by husbands:

- Smoother-feeling skin
- Noticeably warmer skin surface
- Change in the color of the vulva (female external genitals)

The Aging-Gamete Theory and NFP

One concern has been voiced about NFP: the possible association between use of the method and birth defects.

It is known from animal studies that if egg or sperm cells are "old," there is a greater incidence of fetal abnormalities and spontaneous abortions. So it has been postulated that if a human conception occurs from a preovulatory inter-course with a sperm cell that has lingered in the reproductive tract too long or from a postovulatory intercourse with an egg cell a few hours too old, the child may suffer birth defects or even be lost through miscarriage.

This happens to be a case in which the evidence from animal studies cannot be extrapolated to humans. Under natural conditions animals permit mating only when they are "in heat." In some species ovulation is triggered by the act of mating itself. Thus, it is *likely* that unnatural experimental manipulation of the time of fertilization would adversely affect animal conceptions and their outcome.

By contrast, the time for human sexual intercourse isn't restricted in any way. And since nature tends to be efficient, it seems unlikely that the age of the gametes is either crucial or even relevant to the health of the offspring.[13]

Discredited Research: But never mind the theory: Researchers have been looking at studies to see if the aging-gamete theory really holds up in humans. The first study conducted by Piet H. Jongbloet claiming that it does has been discredited worldwide.

Jongbloet looked at the incidences of mental retardation in a little town in Holland. By questioning the parents concerning where the mother had been in her cycle when pregnancy occurred—questioning that was, in some cases, conducted years after the birth—Jongbloet concluded that a possible cause of the retardation was the aging of the sperm or of the egg.

There are several problems with Jongbloet's research. First: How could parents remember, *years after the fact,* the circumstances surrounding the conception of their retarded children? Accurate information would be possible only if the mothers had maintained careful charts on their fertility signs, both temperature and mucus. These parents had not.

Another problem: Jongbloet showed that the average maternal age of the mothers whose children were retarded was substantially higher than that of the mothers whose children were normal. ". . . Since the incidence of Down's syndrome increases with age, this could confound the apparent association if most 'abnormal' progeny were borne by older women," reports Dr. R. H. Gray, professor and chairman of the Johns Hopkins University School of Hygiene and Public Health.

These and other criticisms have been leveled against Jongbloet's study, prompting Dr. Gray to conclude: ". . . the data provided by Jongbloet are scientifically unsound and in the absence of supporting information from other studies these findings do not indicate a higher risk of mental retardation among pregnancies due to NFP method failures."[14]

Continuing Research Efforts: It should be noted that several research efforts have been made in this area. "The association between practice of NFP and birth defects has never been substantiated to my satisfaction," said Dr. Gabriel Bialy, chief of contraceptive research, National Institute of Child Health and Human Development. "In a study conducted by us on rates of congenital anomalies among offspring of contraceptive users, we did not see an excess of anomalies among 'rhythm' users. . . . In the Los Angeles [Cedars-Sinai] study that was sponsored by us, we did not observe either an increased rate of spontaneous abortions or of congenital anomalies among couples using NFP methods."[15]

A study conducted by Michael B. Bracken and Kathy Vita for Yale University's Department of Epidemiology and Public Health showed that NFP was not associated with an increased risk of birth defects in general, but there was an increased risk for some groups of defects, specifically for cleft lip and palate and for congenital hydrocele. But even these defects pose a problem: These conditions occur relatively late in gestation. Thus, so-called aging gametes are almost certainly not their cause. So why the greater incidence of these abnormalities among NFP parents? "It is most likely that these are chance findings . . . ," the researchers report.[16]

One study did show a modest, but statistically insignificant, connection between NFP-related pregnancies and serious birth defects: 5.14 percent for women using NFP as compared to 4.73 percent for women who conceived while not using contraception. On the other hand, the same study showed that only 5.08 percent of NFP mothers' children were of low birth weight as compared to 7.20 percent of noncontraceptors.[17] Other researchers point out that conclusions cannot really be drawn inasmuch as this study made no adjustment for variables such as maternal age, which could explain both birth defects and low birth weight.

Coming to Conclusions: How should all of the evidence concerning use of NFP and possible birth defects be considered, pro and con? "The data simply are not convincing one way or the other," report veteran birth control researchers Hatcher, Guest, Trussell, Frank, Stewart, and Stewart. "If, indeed, there is an increased risk of abnormal offspring when failures occur, it is of a low magnitude."[18]

An International Planned Parenthood Federation publication makes essentially the same point:

> While the possibility that periodic abstinence may be associated with a higher incidence of spontaneous abortion and congenital defects in the offspring should be the subject of further study, the present evidence does not suggest that the risk, if any, is appreciable. There is, therefore, no more need to warn prospective users of this hypothetical risk than there would be when prescribing a vaginal spermicide.[19]

4

✧✦✧✦✧✦✧✦✧

New Dimensions in Sexuality

I have attended any number of medical seminars on contraception. Something jumps out with sore-thumb prominence at all of these presentations: the fact that I almost never hear the words "man," "husband," "partner," or "spouse" more than once for every five hundred or so times I hear the word "woman."

This view is lopsided because, in actual fact, *fertility is a shared condition.*

This understanding explains an awareness held by natural family planning providers: the awareness that they are dealing with considerably more than a birth control method. First of all, *both* the man and the woman must agree to use the method and must thereafter remain cooperative partners in the venture. Thus, the primary focus of natural methods is a couple—not a device or a chemical. Moreover, for NFP to be effective, the behavior of two individuals must be modified—not the body of one of the pair.

Use of natural family planning makes it possible for a man to develop a deeper awareness of his own reproductive power, an assist that he needs more than a woman, since a woman's reproductive experience is continuous.

For example, a woman may experience sexual intercourse followed by the growth of a child within her body, then birth, then very likely breast-feeding. Barbara Grizzuti Harrison writes about her daughter Anna's observation on the subject: "Women bring past, present and future to sex: their deeply embedded biological coding as well as their emotional histories. For women, every act of lovemaking embodies the mystery, or the memory, of life growing from the act."[1]

Even without a mate, a woman still experiences the normal unfolding of her menstrual cycle, a continuous reminder of her reproductive potential. By contrast, a man has little to remind him of his own creative potential. In the absence of an ongoing genital relationship, a man may experience erections and nocturnal emissions (so-called wet dreams), but these are strong genital/sexual responses and urges. Few men relate these experiences to their powerful possibility of bringing forth life.

Lovemaking with the mutual intention of conceiving can help to bring a man more in touch with his life-giving potential. But if there are serious reasons to avoid pregnancy, the choice to *defer* a potentially life-giving act also powerfully underscores for a man the reality of his fertility. Many men have reported profound gratitude for this awareness:

> My attitude toward everything concerning sex, birth control, and pregnancy was that my wife and her gynecologist could decide everything and my wife could let me know what they had decided. So when we first switched to NFP I didn't like the fact that I had to be involved in the decision-making. But gradually my feelings have changed. Today I'm amazed that for so long I stayed on the outside of such important matters affecting our family.

Another husband had a different experience:

> When my wife accidentally got pregnant while using the diaphragm, I blamed her. And that's the right word: blame.
>
> In those days, I never thought about my fertility very much one way or another. When we started using NFP, I became much more aware of the fact that something *I* contributed could cause another child. The first time it hit me, I was deeply moved. Awed, really. Ever since, something has changed in me for the better. My wife and I both agree on this change in me, by the way.

It is important to point out that the deferred act is not a negative, in the sense that "nothing happened." Rather, *the deferred act of lovemaking is a positive affirmation of the sweep and power of the couple's creative potential.* It is only with respectful recognition of that creative potential— and even a sense of wonder and awe that it exists—that the couple defers.

None of this is to say that the use of natural methods is inherently easy. For some it is too demanding. "If a couple always has to run to a chart to find out whether or not they can make love, their expression becomes stilted and unnatural," one woman complained. "That's why I believe that natural methods are really *unnatural*. They interfere with a couple's spontaneity."

This woman is not alone in viewing the self-imposed restriction of intercourse to the infertile time as unnatural. Some have even suggested that artificial methods, particularly the Pill, the IUD, and sterilization, are more "natural" because they make it possible for a woman to express her sexual urges at will or to respond to her husband's at any time without fear of pregnancy.

But there is a problem with this idea: It suggests that the essence of the natural in human behavior is to express every urge felt, when felt, without consideration for the possible consequences. Obviously, this type of behavior doesn't conform with our rationality. And as far as NFP is concerned, most couples using it have sensitively and thoughtfully integrated their impulsive sexual selves with their rational ("We have important reasons to avoid pregnancy") selves. What's more, there are benefits for the couple making the effort to make this integration.

One benefit is that NFP helps to uncover new dimensions in the male-female sexual relationship. For example, many couples are surprised that a short abstinence phase seems to enhance, not detract from, the relationship. Dr. David E. Landers, of Teaneck, New Jersey, an obstetrician and gynecologist with a deep interest in natural family planning, offers one explanation for this enhancement factor.

According to Dr. Landers, the primitive biological urge, human sexual energy, can be "harnessed" by us. Once harnessed, it can then be used to express whatever we want it to express, ideally love, joy, tenderness, empathy—all the positive human emotions.

Abstinence actively helps to harness this energy. Like any energy source, sexual energy is more effective if "stored," to be released later at an appropriate time of our choice.

Sexual energy release is most readily triggered by the erotic. But that is also the most superficial "trigger." According to Dr. Landers, periodic abstinence helps the couple grow so that ultimately the "triggers" releasing sexual energy become the emotional and affective aspects of the couple's love bond. As a result, the erotic gradually loses its position as the primary sexual force. Instead, the *other person,* the loved one, plus the emotions and feelings felt toward the loved one, becomes the primary force. Thus, the couple's life *together*—their joys, shared difficulties, achievements and milestones, headaches and heartaches—these life experiences can become the "power centers" of the sexual relationship.

Eventually, "person-centered" sexuality becomes a new

sexual behavior pattern. But unlike the primitive sexual urge, it is *not* an instinctive behavior pattern: It must be learned. Moreover, the learning depends on sexual energy control.

Certainly one reason so many have become enthusiastic about NFP is that they have begun to master the art of sexual energy control. One woman commented on the positive effects on her marriage:

> When we *can* make love, my husband is more affectionate and tender and gentle. He is affectionate every day and looks forward to when we can make love. I don't feel "used" anymore and know he doesn't take advantage of sex *or* me.

Dr. James Fox, also a gynecologist-obstetrician practicing in Teaneck, New Jersey, points out other aspects of natural family planning. According to Dr. Fox, NFP is a method that operates simultaneously on at least three levels: the technological, the physical, and the interpersonal.

The Technological Level: Like the really effective contraceptive methods, natural family planning is highly reliable when used properly. Unplanned pregnancies are rare, and at the same time, the method has no verifiable hazardous side effects. In other words, from the point of view of sheer "technology" the method *works,* it is effective.

The Physical Level: I never interviewed an individual or a couple who complained that their sexual relationship had deteriorated because of their acceptance of abstinence. This complaint did appear twice in the questionnaires, but couples overwhelmingly reported that their physical relationship had improved, sometimes considerably, since relying on NFP. This husband's comment is typical:

> The abstinence period intensifies my yearning for my wife. By the time we can have intercourse again, she's been constantly in my mind for days. I have found that because of this,

now I love her more and I also love making love to her more. We both look forward to our "honeymoon" night with longing and excitement.

Certainly one reason most couples' physical relationship tends to improve is that the pair are "storing" their sexual energies. As one woman married less than a year said, "Abstinence is the best aphrodisiac." Obviously, contraception doesn't involve any kind of storage and may be a factor in the growing problems of sexual boredom, lack of sexual desire, and male impotence.

Another matter: Women often felt "used" while using contraceptives, particularly since many husbands tended to forget about "courting" them. Once they learned that their husbands were willing to abstain for a short period of time—in effect, not "use" them; rather, court them—their responses became more ardent when intercourse became available again.

The Interpersonal Level: The human sexual experience is never wholly separated from the personal experience. Moreover, there are many ways to use sexual intercourse. It can be used for exploitation, conquest, humiliation, anger, etc.

There are other uses for sex. "In addition to sex for procreation and sex for pleasure, we have sex for solving the problems of confused identity and low self-worth," reports psychiatrist Abraham J. Twerski, M.D. "Physiologically, sex is well suited to accomplish the first two goals, but when it is pressed into service of the third it becomes subject to all types of distortion."[2]

While sexual intercourse can be misused, ideally it should be an expression of the deeper human emotions. Love, joy, spiritual closeness, tenderness, and other deep emotions that move men and women are profoundly suitable for sexual expression, although this is by no means the exclusive, or even the best, mode of expression. A touch, a glance, or a soft smile may say considerably more.

Most couples understand this instinctively. Still, this instinctive understanding may be one reason why couples are willing to walk into an NFP class: They already know that abstinence will be involved, but their values are sufficiently developed that "sex on demand" is no longer an essential value to them. It may still be *important*—and a cause of early difficulties using natural family planning— but it is no longer an *essential* value.

A young husband's experience shows how he and his wife began to experience natural family planning at all its levels:

> I never thought that after ten years of marriage and a handful of children I would ever feel the yearning for my wife that I felt when we courted and were first married. I figured that all those old feelings were a part of being young and in love. Being older and loving each other was nice, but there certainly wasn't any cha-cha-cha about it.
>
> I wasn't enthusiastic when we changed to NFP, but we saw no other way. We went to class very, very reluctantly. Me especially.
>
> But almost right away it started happening again: that incredible yearning I used to feel for my wife returned—and not just once in a while: It was there every month. Every cycle gradually turned into courtship and honeymoon all over again.
>
> We think that the longing and yearning we feel for each other is better than what we felt when we were younger. We both think this is because we've been through so much together by now—childbirth, baby's first steps, family weddings, as well as unemployment, sickness, and other hard times. NFP has become more than a method of birth control for us: It's a lifestyle.

A woman was ebullient in summarizing her experience of NFP in the couple's life:

Our marriage "began" and bloomed 100 percent after we started using NFP. We felt closer to God and this helped our marriage. We had the phases of courtship and honeymoon and celebrated. We shared my body awareness. We shared days of uncertainty and we shared days of gambling and pregnancy. It was a change from "I" to "we." Our last baby was conceived out of love, and with full knowledge that we would conceive. From that moment we could picture the hours and days of growth.

But before NFP I *feared* going to bed, as I didn't know my fertility cycle and worried that I might become pregnant. Now I know my fertility signs and feel 100 percent confident in those signs and no longer fear. It is a great relief and a burden off my shoulders. I want more children—but when I am ready and capable.

I would like to make a personal comment at this time. When I first learned about natural family planning, I thought of it as a last resort for couples who simply could not tolerate (for reasons of health) the effective artificial methods. And except for those with moral objections to contraception, it was unimaginable to me that any couple would actually *prefer* a natural method to an artificial one.

Today I recognize that periodic abstinence is not only effective for fertility control, it is also a creative contribution to the human experience. It is my hope that this aspect of natural family planning will become your discovery, too.

5

❖❖❖❖❖❖❖

Infertility
and the Delayed
Childbearing Decision

With so many articles and books written about avoiding pregnancy, it is easy to forget that there is a growing minority with a different problem: couples who want to get pregnant and can't. As a matter of record, experts agree that the problem of infertility is worsening. Today it is estimated that as many as one out of eight to ten couples is having difficulty achieving a desired pregnancy.

Statistically, about a third of all infertile couples are unable to conceive because the woman doesn't ovulate. A period of months spent eating nutritiously and taking supplements (especially the B-complex nutrients, vitamins C, D, E, and A, plus some of the minerals) may help stimulate ovulation again. This is particularly the case if an inability to ovulate is related to prior Pill use. It is recognized that oral contraceptives deplete certain essential nutrients.

Of course, not all ovulatory problems result from contraceptive use or poor health. A preexisting problem may prevent ovulation because of some unknown cause. If you have a preexisting problem and are taking the Pill or are using an IUD, *you are exposing yourself to birth control hazards that are completely unnecessary, since you can't conceive in the first place.* Worse, you might compound a possible fertility problem through use of either of those contraceptive measures. If you are using barrier methods, the contraceptives are unnecessarily interrupting every act of intercourse to "prevent" a conception that can't occur anyway.

Now consider the difference if you use fertility awareness methods. If you take your temperature every morning and discover no rise, or if you observed that sometimes there are bleeding episodes that are not preceded by a rise, you are alerted to a future problem relatively early in your marriage. What's more, you are alerted to this problem *while your youth is on your side.*

It is also worth noting that there is a great deal of research going on to develop a device, a simple test—*something* that will signal that ovulation is pending. If reliable, such products could be valuable adjuncts in using fertility awareness methods.

In contrast, couples with ovulatory difficulties who use artificial methods may not discover potential problems until at least a year or more *after* they have decided they want to achieve a pregnancy. Depending on how long they delayed pregnancy, any number of years could pass before they are abruptly made aware of the fact that they may not be able to conceive very readily—indeed, that they probably never *were* able to conceive very readily.

For these reasons, among others, many infertility experts urge couples not to delay childbearing. Instead, couples should ask themselves, "How old will we be when our last child is born?" It is preferable for a woman to be in her early thirties when the last child is born rather than bearing her first at that age. Remember: There is only one day in your cycle when you can possibly conceive, so you have an average of approximately eleven to fourteen opportunities in one year to achieve conception. If childbearing is delayed, it is possible that all the opportunities to conceive within one year will be expended before you even begin to realize that you *have* a problem.

Once you recognize that there is a difficulty and begin your visits to a doctor who might be able to help, additional opportunities to conceive will pass as the physician works to assess the problem. Meanwhile, you are growing older and your options are narrowing apace.

So if you are delaying a pregnancy, natural family planning is the best means for delay. NFP is as effective as the Pill and surgical sterilization (and more effective than any of the other methods), but it poses no risk whatsoever to either your health or your future fertility.

There is more: NFP can give you a slight time advantage on the first visit to a specialist if you suspect that you have an infertility problem. Since ovulation is essential to conception, your doctor is going to want to find out if you are ovulating. Don't *tell* the physician that you have or have not been ovulating; *show* the evidence. Come for that first visit with all your charts in hand. If your doctor is satisfied with the evidence, it will be possible to advance more quickly to other diagnostic tests to evaluate other possible causes of infertility. This is not a trivial point: At this juncture in your life, time is important.

But even before spending time and money to see a doctor, NFP awareness helps many couples to achieve a desired conception, as the following three case histories show:

Case #1: Lorraine and Bob (none of these are the couples' real names) had been unable to achieve pregnancy for nearly two years. They learned why after their second class of NFP instruction. Unwittingly, they never had relations during the fertile time. Reason? Lorraine felt achy and bloated around the time of ovulation—*her* individual fertility sign. Bur Lorraine conceived without difficulty from a single act of coitus during the (uncomfortable) fertile time.

Case #2: Gail and David were unable to conceive for several years after "trying very hard." Upon questioning, the doctor learned that the pair had been trying very hard indeed: They had relations every day of the cycle except the days of menstruation. The doctor suspected that such frequency of intercourse was keeping the sperm count too low to achieve conception.

Gail was taught to observe the changes in her cervical mucus, and she and David began abstaining to build the supply of fresh, viable sperm. Abstinence ended the day Gail noticed the slippery sensation of raw-egg-white mucus in her genital area. They conceived in the first cycle.

Case #3: Jayne and Neil had not conceived their first two children very readily and were concerned that after nearly twenty months their third still hadn't been conceived. Once the couple learned fertility awareness, they realized that Neil's traveling job found him to be away from home during almost every fertile phase. Solution? The two children were sent to Grannie's for a four-day visit while Jayne went on the business trip with Neil. Jayne didn't conceive on the first trip, but she did on the second.

It is important to underscore the fact that these couples didn't really have any *infertility* problems, only *timing* problems. And sometimes the matter of timing can be very delicate indeed. Remember that the couple, *as a unit,* is fertile. As Lester B. Anderman, M.D., of Los Angeles, points out, a couple's fertility is made up of the relative fertility potential of each partner. Thus, a wife with a high potential may compensate for a husband with a lower potential and vice versa, and in such cases, *timing is all,*as this excerpt from a forty-one-year-old registered nurse's letter makes clear:

I have tried for years to achieve a pregnancy. Our boy is adopted. I'm weary of seeking help through gynecologists; it's expensive, sometimes humiliating, and it's depressing never to achieve.

Although I was seen at an infertility clinic at a university hospital and have been on fertility drugs for years, *no one* taught me what NFP did. I feel that if I had only been taught this—how to tell when I ovulate—maybe I would have achieved that wanted pregnancy. Because my husband's sperm count is low, but supposedly adequate, and because I was on fertility drugs, timing was all-important. But we never knew on which day I ovulated. NFP has an important story to tell.

I don't know whether she ever did conceive—she wrote to me anonymously—but she is right: NFP *does* have an important story to tell.

There is an additional bonus to using timed acts of intercourse in conjuction with NFP awareness to achieve a pregnancy. If you conceive, you may want to invest in one of those home pregnancy tests, which are now quite reliable, but don't forget that you can also be 99 percent sure of pregnancy if your waking temperature remains elevated seven days beyond your norm and you haven't menstruated. Either way—by checking a home pregnancy test or your elevated temperature—you will be able to switch roles with your physician: Give the doctor the good news!

PART TWO

∘⟨∘⟩∘⟨∘⟩∘

How to
Start Charting
Tomorrow

6

✵✧✵✧✵✧✵

How to Chart
Your First and
Second Cycles

Before you begin charting your cycles, there is one essential point that you must always bear in mind: Natural family planning information helps you only to *bracket* your fertile time. *It gives you no information whatsoever about the day you will ovulate or the day you have ovulated.*

Since there is no way to know with certainty when ovulation has taken place or will take place, you must presume fertility on every single day of your fertile phase. Do not attempt to second-guess the guidelines and do *not* take chances. This couple's experience is instructive:

> As young newlyweds with nothing in the bank and plenty of school loans to pay off, we felt that it was very important to avoid pregnancy for at least two years. But after we had been using NFP for a year we felt *very* confident. It was our anniversary and we felt that we could cut one day, just one measly day, from Jan's fertile time. Well, that was quite a celebration: It brought us David nine months later.

We are thrilled with our baby and delighted *now* that we took the chance *then,* although when we first learned that Jan was pregnant, we were both very upset.

We have continued using NFP since David's birth, but believe me: *We don't cut corners.* If the guidelines say that Jan is fertile, *she's fertile.*

I would also urge you to seek competent *personal* instruction. To be sure, I have met many couples who have learned to practice natural family planning from how-to books alone. Still, I think that personal guidance is valuable. For this reason the appendix lists referral addresses of teaching couples and centers throughout the United States and Canada.

If there is no way for you to get personal instruction, *follow this book carefully.* It has been designed to be completely self-instructional. Both partners should read all of part 1 and the relevant portions of part 2.

As for charting, it takes far less time than inserting a diaphragm and at the same time offers potential for communication. For one couple it is a positive experience that they deliberately take time to enjoy:

> We've tried to keep up a daily dialogue. Our charting allows us a very special five to ten minutes during the day to discuss our personal and sexual feelings and their causes. We've always been an open, loving, touching couple—but stress of everyday life can hinder this. Charting helps us to grow!

It is up to the couple to decide who will handle the charting, of course, but my recommendation is that the man take charge of it. Personal and sexual communication is usually better when men handle it. So is charting. As one wife told me: "He asks, 'Do you mean somewhat translucent or actually clear mucus?' I'm forced to define the mucus change more precisely. The fact that my husband is 'on the team' really helps." One husband took such complete responsibility that his wife's gynecologist had to telephone him during a routine examination to find out when her next menstrual period was due!

Once you learn how to chart signs and how to recognize the fertile and infertile phases, you will be able to sever yourselves completely from the doctor and/or the drugstore in handling your family planning responsibilities. Above all, natural family planning is *personal* control.

There is a blank chart in the back of his book. Photocopy it and begin using the copies to chart your fertile signs.

For "Recorded cycle number," begin with "1." Continue with each successive recorded cycle ("2," "3," "4," etc.). Get in the habit of keeping careful records and save all your charts. Then as your cycles pass, one after another, you will begin to see *your* personal fertility picture emerge.

Getting Started

You can begin your practice of natural family planning at this moment. In doing so, there is only one "rule" to keep in mind, and it *always* applies:

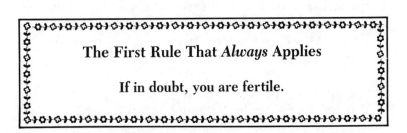

The First Rule That *Always* Applies

If in doubt, you are fertile.

If you follow this important rule, you won't have to worry about an error in determining your fertile time. This is because you must consider yourself fertile *until you can prove that you are infertile.* Thus, *at this moment,* you must consider yourself fertile.

The Second Rule That *Always* Applies

If you wish to avoid pregnancy, not even a drop of semen can come in contact with the female external genitals during the fertile time. This requirement rules out not only sexual intercourse but also all genital-genital contact until the couple can prove infertility.

"Proof" of Infertility: What constitutes proof of infertility? When you are beginning, the only positive proof of infertility is a *sustained basal body temperature rise* according to a specific formula: the rule of "3 and 2 and 6." (This rule will be explained in a moment.)

Some women experience so-called intermenstrual bleeding episodes. These bleedings do *not* follow ovulation. They occur because the uterine lining breaks down for some reason, usually due to a decrease in estrogen or progesterone production. Indeed, it is possible to ovulate and thus conceive during such a bleeding. *So UNLESS the couple is checking temperature to confirm the return of infertility, any bleeding experienced by the woman must always be considered fertile.* Only a previous sustained temperature rise can prove otherwise.

You will be using the "3 and 2 and 6" formula during your first two learning cycles. Later, you will learn to chart the cervical mucus changes, evaluating two indicators according to the guidelines Dr. Roetzer has devised. With two fertility signs to cross-check, it will be possible to determine infertility earlier in most—but not all—charts. But before moving ahead, it is essential to get a good foundation in temperature-taking. Here is the important background information you require:

Taking Your Temperature: Your *waking* temperature is really what is meant by the term "basal body temperature." You should have at least three hours sleep before taking it, and it should be taken immediately when you awake.

Your Thermometer: Do not use a regular fever thermometer. Buy a BBT (basal body temperature) thermometer at your drugstore. They cost about five or six dollars. A BBT thermometer is much more accurate, and the numbers are bigger and easier to read. Do not use a BBT thermometer if you suspect you have a fever (more about fevers in the following chapter) and never wash it in anything but *cool* water.

How to Take Your Temperature: You can take your temperature orally, rectally, or vaginally. You must, however, be consistent in *each* cycle. Thus, if you start with oral readings at the beginning of your cycle, don't switch to vaginal or rectal readings later in the *same* cycle. Generally, these readings are a bit higher than the oral ones. You still get the same rising *pattern,* of course, no matter which orifice you use. Just use the same one in each cycle.

How to Take Oral Temperature: Oral temperatures should be taken for a full eight to ten minutes to ensure an accurate reading on your BBT thermometer. Do not smoke or drink before taking your temperature; the temperature in your mouth can be affected, which may distort the reading.

On the other hand, do not worry if you happen to wake up an hour early, drink a glass of water, and return to bed. By the time you take your temperature, enough time will have elapsed so that the thermometer will reflect a proper waking temperature provided you take your temperature for the full ten minutes.

You can also feel free to get up and begin your morning routine while taking your oral temperature.

How to Take Vaginal and Rectal Temperatures: Lie in bed on your side in a S-shape to take vaginal or rectal temperatures.

Sometimes Vaseline or some other lubricant may be needed to slide the thermometer into the rectum. Use whatever seems best.

Rectal and vaginal temperatures need to be taken for only five minutes to ensure accurate readings.

Temperature-Taking and Napping: Many women like to nap for the duration of temperature-taking. I urge you to stay awake; you do *not* want your thermometer to break.

If you should happen to fall asleep, you may wind up taking your temperature for a much longer period than usual. This won't affect the reading, according to Dr. Edward F. Keefe, developer of the Ovulindex thermometer, but the risk of breakage does remain.

One couple cuts the risk by keeping an ordinary kitchen timer next to their alarm clock. After the alarm wakens them, they set the timer for the five minutes of temperature-taking. This couple follows the same routine on mornings when they sleep late, waking for temperature-taking, then returning to sleep, so that the temperature is always taken at the same time.

Keeping a Record: After you have taken your temperature, the reading must be recorded on a chart.

Many husbands who handle the charting take care of it at night. If you choose to do it that way, be sure of one thing: Set the thermometer aside somewhere where *it won't be exposed to heat.* Keep it away from a radio, electric light or clock, radiator, etc.

After the temperature has been recorded, always shake down the thermometer. Grasp it near the end where the numbers are highest, hold tight, and give four or five good shakes to make sure that the mercury slides back down toward the bulb.

It is best to shake down the thermometer the preceding night so that it will be ready for you in the morning.

What Readings to Expect: This book will rely on Fahrenheit (F.) temperature measurements rather than centigrade (C.). Most women have a waking oral temperature of about 97.3° before ovulation. Still, don't be surprised if your waking temperature is as low as 96.7° or as high as 97.7°. (And remember: Rectal and vaginal temperatures are generally higher than oral, sometimes as much as a degree higher.)

You may record a temperature that falls between two numbers. If so, the rule is: *Always* record the *lower* temperature. Example: If the mercury stops between 97.7° and 97.8°, record 97.7°.

Disturbances: Take your temperature at the same time each morning. If you take it forty-five minutes to an hour or more later than usual, make a notation to this effect on your chart. Usually, the reading is about 0.1° higher for each hour later.

You can also expect (and should make note of) higher than normal temperatures if you experienced any of the following conditions:

- Slept restlessly
- Were wakened several times during the night ("restless night")
- Had several alcoholic drinks the night before (and usually don't)
- Are taking special medication (especially hormonal-type medication)
- Are under severe emotional stress
- Are ill
- Used an electric blanket

Such situations are known as disturbances. I will explain what to do about them a little later.

Charting the First and Second Cycles

You are fertile until you can prove otherwise. For your first two cycles the only reliable proof of infertility is the temperature rise according to the "3 and 2 and 6" Guideline.

Recall that after you ovulate, the ovarian sac that contained the egg begins releasing additional progesterone into your system. Progesterone is a heat-producing hormone, which is why you can observe a temperature rise.

Over the years many formulations have been created to define a valid temperature rise. Some involve making averages of all the low temperatures; others involve making a so-called cover line and then checking for high temperatures over that line. Whatever the temperature-rule formulation, it is important that it achieve two goals at once: give accurate information about infertility as early as possible *and* be easy to apply.

In 1937 Dr. J. G. H. Holt published a temperature rule that enjoys the virtue of simplicity and has stood the test of time. The "3 and 2 and 6" Guideline is an adaptation and you are very unlikely to conceive by following it. *But if it is extra important that a pregnancy not occur, a life-and-death matter, add one more high temperature day.* This extra day is a precaution against any mistaken interpretation of the guideline.

"3 and 2 and 6" Guideline

You are infertile after 8:00 P.M. on the day that you have recorded *THREE* consecutive temperatures at least *0.2°* higher than the highest of the *SIX* lowest consecutive temperatures recorded just before the rise begins.

The beginning of the rise is identified when you observe one temperature higher than the preceding six. (Note: The temperature does not have to be 0.2° higher.) Eliminate any "disturbed" temperatures when making this evaluation.

Once the rise is identified, you are looking for two sets of temperatures: a consecutive low set followed by a consecutive high set. *All three temperatures* of the high set must be at least 0.2° higher than the highest reading of the six low temperatures.

Once proved, infertility continues from 8:00 P.M. through day 5 of the succeeding cycle. There is one exception to this: If you have ever experienced cycles of 22 days or *less,* presume fertility starting on day 1 of the next cycle.

Ovulation occurs sometime between the 12th and 16th days prior to menstruation. (See information about the 21-Day Rule at the end of this chapter for possible exceptions.) To show this, do a reverse 1 to 16 count at the end of each cycle. This count-back is entered beneath the cycle days and will point up the consistency between the temperature rise and the probable time of ovulation.

Chart No. 1—Typical Temperature: You can see how the guideline can be applied in three easy steps to Amy's 33-day cycle.

1. *Identify the start of the rise.*

   Amy identifies the start when one temperature higher than the preceding lowest consecutive six is observed. For Amy it is the temperature on cycle day 20.

2. *Number in reverse the six consecutive low temperatures just before the rise and draw a line across the highest.*

   Amy's six consecutive low temperatures just before the rise occur on days 14 through 19; the highest occurs (twice) at 97.6°, where the "low set" line is drawn.

3. *Draw a line 0.2° above the first line and circle three consecutive temperatures that fall ON or ABOVE this line.*

   Amy's three consecutive high temperatures occur on days 21, 22, and 23.

Amy proves infertility on the third high temperature day (day 23). It lasts from 8:00 P.M. on that day through at least the first 5 days of the next cycle.

Amy's 1 to 16 count-back shows that she ovulated sometime between days 18 and 22. In this, and in all succeeding charts, the 12 through 16 count-back days are screened to show you the coincidence between the fertility signs and the probable time of ovulation.

CHART NO. 1:
Typical Temperature

PERSONAL FERTILITY CHART

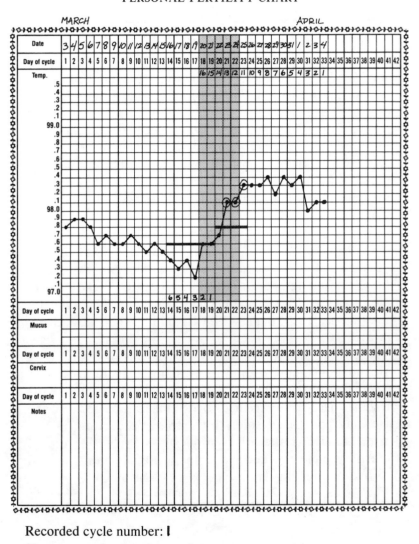

Recorded cycle number: **1**

Shortest previous cycle: days

Number of days in this cycle: **33** days

Chart No. 2—Temperature Disturbances: Earlier in this chapter I pointed out that you may record higher than normal waking temperatures if you were ill, had a few alcoholic drinks the night before and usually don't, slept very late, and so on.

If you record a high temperature that is clearly caused by a disturbance, *disregard the temperature.* Just skip over that day's count and continue your count the following day. There is further information about such situations in the next chapter. Meanwhile, Jane's chart will clarify most charting questions.

Jane has two temperature disturbances. She disregards the disturbed temperature among the "low set" ("Slept late"), as you can see by the count. The disturbed temperature among the "high set" ("Drinking!") is also disregarded.

Regarding the latter: It *is* the day after New Year's Eve! Alcohol consumption can raise waking temperatures a bit, especially for the occasional drinker. Although she records it, Jane disregards the disturbed temperature because the rise may be caused solely by extraneous factors (in this case, alcohol) rather than progesterone. To be sure of infertility, Jane checked the temperature one more day and "proved" infertility on cycle day 24 (January 2).

CHART NO. 2:
Temperature Disturbances

PERSONAL FERTILITY CHART

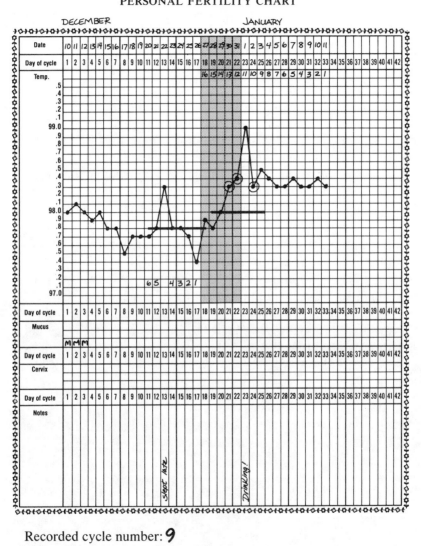

Recorded cycle number: **9**
Shortest previous cycle: **30** days
Number of days in this cycle: **33** days

Chart No. 3—Gradual Rise and Temperature Dip: Leslie's chart shows a very gradual temperature rise. In addition, one of her high readings (day 22) dips *below* the "high set" line.

Remember: It is necessary to look for three *consecutive* high temperatures. As discussed on chart no. 2, if you have a high temperature disturbance, you can skip the temperature and continue your count the following day. But if you experience a temperature *dip* bringing you *below* your "high set" line, you must *begin* the high set count anew.

As you can see on this chart, Leslie's day 22 temperature dip made it necessary for her to begin her count a second time, starting on day 23. She proved infertility three days later, on day 25.

CHART NO. 3:
Gradual Rise and Temperature Dip

PERSONAL FERTILITY CHART

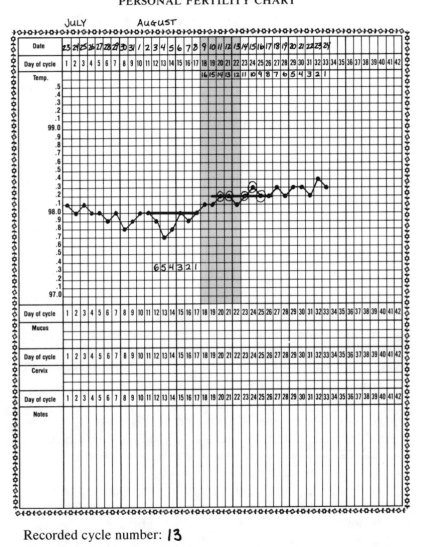

Recorded cycle number: **13**
Shortest previous cycle: **32** days
Number of days in this cycle: **33** days

Bleeding and the "3 and 2 and 6" Guideline: If you don't notice a temperature rise (which indicates ovulation) and bleeding begins, *you must still consider yourself fertile through the duration of any bleeding episode.* It is *not* a true menstruation, since ovulation did not precede it. Intermenstrual bleedings may be precipitated by a drop in circulating estrogen, *not* by ovulation. Moreover, if you did not ovulate prior to the bleeding episode, it is possible to ovulate—and thus to conceive—*during* the bleeding. So *unless you are checking temperatures to confirm the return of infertility, you must consider any bleeding episode to be fertile.* Only a sustained temperature rise can prove otherwise.

What If You Don't "Prove" Infertility? You may experience a rise so shallow that it does not satisfy the requirements of the "3 and 2 and 6" Guideline. If this happens, you won't be able to "prove" infertility. What should you do?

If you have not been able to find NFP instruction in your area and must rely solely on the information contained in this book, then you must presume fertility even in the face of a shallow temperature rise if it doesn't fulfill the requirements of the "3 and 2 and 6" Guideline. Fertility continues through any bleeding episode that occurs.

You may, or may not, be in a new cycle after a bleeding episode that follows a shallow temperature rise. (Since the episode isn't defined as menstrual, the first day of bleeding can't be defined as the first day of a new cycle either.) If you feel confident that you can observe and distinguish mucus changes, you may follow the guidelines for charting the third and fourth cycles after a bleeding episode. If you are not confident about your ability to chart mucus, you are "in doubt"—*and fertile.* Fertility lasts until an appropriate temperature rise is (finally!) recorded according to the "3 and 2 and 6" Guideline.

A man is fertile every single day. For an indefinite time a woman will also be "fertile" on a daily basis. It is a new situation. A great deal of couple communication, sharing, and mutual agreement is demanded. While difficult, in a very real sense this situation is an *opportunity*.

In this connection every NFP teaching couple has special memories of certain couples they have helped. One of these fondly remembered couples was a young post-Pill pair with a special story about abstinence. It was the worst story I had ever heard . . . and the best.

They were young—about eighteen and nineteen—and had been married about a year. She had been on the Pill the whole time, but something about it bothered her deeply. She said that she felt it was wrong to be using it, although neither of them held religious beliefs on the matter. Since it meant a lot to her to stop using an artificial method, her husband willingly agreed to learn a natural one.

They came to our class and everything seemed to be going fine. Then they missed a session and we wondered if something was wrong. I called and he answered the phone. He was quite brusque. "No, there's nothing wrong, good-bye." That was the conversation.

Something was wrong, so I asked my wife to reach his wife. She did, and sure enough, there were problems. It looked as though there might be a layoff and he'd be out of work; a drummer had moved in upstairs and practiced constantly; *and* they were in their third month of complete abstinence.

Naturally, we made an immediate appointment. They brought all their charts, and the four of us sat down together. I figured out where the couple had gone off the track on their charting and was able to show them days they could have made love. Those months of abstinence would have been unnecessary if they had only called us!

The two were visibly relieved to learn that they had been mistaken in their charting and that abstinence was coming to an end. I found myself apologizing that they had gone through such a rough time together. But she stopped me dead in midsentence. I'll never forget her words: "Don't! Don't apologize. The abstinence was hard, but I wouldn't have traded it for anything in this whole world. Nothing.

"When you get married, you don't really know how it's going to work out. You can't be sure if love will be there six months later, much less for good. But I'll tell you one thing that I now know without the slightest doubt: *I am loved.* And I also know that *we love each other.* These three months have been the most important of our lives. Because of them, we learned that we're in love for today—and for always."

Mucus Changes

Besides checking for the temperature rise during your first two learning cycles, you should start developing your mucus awareness. Don't worry about recording the mucus changes—the observation is too new for you to be able to begin charting it right now—just start working on your *awareness*.

Some women, of course, worry that they won't be able to notice the changes. If this is your worry, here are some useful hints:

- Avoid synthetic fibers. They can cause a false sensation of moistness due to the fact that the fibers don't "breathe" as natural ones do. So stick to cotton underwear, including panty hose with cotton crotch.
- Tight-fitting shorts, slacks, jeans, etc. which cut close at the crotch and press close at the vaginal entrance may cause an artificial moistness that makes it difficult to interpret mucus. Try wearing skirts and dresses for a while until you learn the sign.
- Many women insert one or two fingers (forefinger and middle finger) into the vagina. For many, this is the best way to check for mucus.
- Check toilet tissue each time you void, both before and after. Slightly less absorbent, cheaper tissue is better than the very soft, perfumed, expensive products.

- Finally, at the beginning, *concentrate!* Surprisingly soon you will get used to the external sensation of mucus *once* you begin concentrating on its existence.

Check for developing mucus each time you go to the bathroom. Wipe yourself before urinating. Do you get the slip-through feeling? Can you actually see mucus? Become alert to the changes, but don't worry about recording them at this point.

When Mucus Observations Are Worthless: You cannot reliably learn the mucus sign if you are using contraceptives. Plan to discontinue their use as you make the switch to natural birth control. Here is a quick rundown on some of the problems they can cause which can interfere with your fertility observations:

- *The Pill:* The hormones may act on and alter cervical mucus.
- *IUD:* Some women experience discharges that conflict with the mucus sign.
- *Diaphragm:* The required creams and jellies often lead to confused interpretation of the mucus sign as well as prompting allergic reactions—and possible discharges—which may aggravate the problem.
- *Foam and vaginal suppositories:* The contraceptives themselves confuse the mucus sign. In addition, they sometimes cause allergic reactions and confusing discharges that add to interpretive difficulties.
- *Condoms:* Both treated and untreated prophylactics cause allergic reactions in some women—and in some men!
- *Sponge:* Allergic reactions have been reported.

Pregnancy and the Use of Barriers: Natural family planning providers report that couples using barrier method contraceptives during the fertile time report "significantly" higher pregnancy rates than couples who abstain, although at this writing there is no controlled study showing precisely how high the rates are.

Why pregnancy rates should be so high for this group is widely discussed in the NFP community. Besides the possible confusion of the mucus sign that frequently occurs when barrier methods are used, two additional reasons have been suggested.

First, could it be that couples who do not intend to abstain are not as careful with their fertility observations as couples who *do* intend to abstain? If so, they may unintentionally fail to use barriers during a time of fertility.

It has also been argued that barrier methods are considerably less reliable than their effectiveness figures suggest. This is because the figures take into account *all* acts of intercourse using a particular contraceptive throughout a cycle—and 80 percent of the cycle is infertile anyway. Those who hold to this view point out that if the use of barriers is restricted to the only time a woman can conceive, higher pregnancy rates must result, since barrier methods aren't that effective *anyway*.

Some hold that all three factors (confused mucus sign, careless fertility observations, relative ineffectiveness of barrier methods) may be involved, depending on the couple and on the circumstances.

Whatever the reason (or reasons) for reduced effectiveness, you should plan to discontinue barrier methods if you want to achieve 99.2 percent NFP reliability. (See Part III for additional reasons.)

Mucus and Disturbed Vaginal Balance: Other "outside interferences" having nothing to do with contraceptives sometimes cause problems in interpreting the mucus sign. Included are tampons (deodorant and plain), vaginal deodorants, and antibiotics. Here is why these products can sometimes cause problems:

The vagina normally contains lactic-acid-forming bacteria essential for self-cleaning. Tampons can absorb these healthy bacteria if your bleeding is very light. As a result, you may become more susceptible to various infections (yeast included). These infections may not only be difficult to treat but can also cause discharges which may confuse the mucus sign.

Deodorant tampons can cause an additional difficulty: The chemicals sometimes cause irritation and allergic reactions.

Vaginal deodorants can cause irritations. Moreover, since a healthy vagina is "self-cleaning," it should not emit an offensive odor, assuming normal, proper bathing of the vulva with ordinary soap products. (Baby soap is ideal.) If you *do* notice an unpleasant odor, it may be an indication of pathology and should be checked by a doctor—*never* "treated" with a deodorant.

It is well recognized that antibiotics kill bacteria—the harmful *and* the healthy varieties. Vaginal yeast infections often follow after a course of antibiotics because so many of the healthy bacteria are destroyed that the infections grow unchecked. If your doctor wants to prescribe an antibiotic for any condition associated with a fever, be sure to ask whether it is absolutely necessary to take the medication. If not, don't.

Antihistamines: You know how effectively antihistamines can dry nasal mucus. There is evidence that they are also effective on cervical mucus. If you use them, exercise extra awareness.

The 21-Day Rule

Some couples rely solely on the temperature rise sign in conjunction with the so-called 21-Day Rule to determine the total time of infertility after ovulation. Thus, they don't chart the mucus and cervical signs.

TABLE 3

MENSTRUAL/POSTMENSTRUAL PHASE	OVULATORY PHASE	POSTOVULATORY PHASE
Couple is infertile	Couple is fertile Conception is likely	Couple is infertile

Day grid (fertile/ovulatory days in **bold**):

1	2	3	4	5	6	7	8	9	10	11	12	13	14	15	16	17	18	19	20	21	22	23	24	25	26	27	28	29	30	31	32	33	34	35	36	37	38	39	40	41	42	43	44
1	2	3	4	5	6	7	8	9	10	11	12	13	14	15	16	17	18	19	20	21	22	23	**24**	**25**	**26**	**27**	**28**	**29**	**30**	**31**	**32**	**33**	34	35	36	37	38	39	40	41	42	43	44
1	2	3	4	5	6	7	8	9	10	11	12	**13**	**14**	**15**	**16**	**17**	**18**	**19**	**20**	**21**	**22**	23	24	25	26	27	28	29	30	31	32	33											
1	2	3	4	5	6	7	8	9	10	11	12	13	14	15	**16**	**17**	**18**	**19**	**20**	**21**	**22**	**23**	**24**	**25**	26	27	28	29	30	31	32	33	34	35	36								
1	2	3	4	5	6	7	8	9	10	11	12	13	14	15	16	17	**18**	**19**	**20**	**21**	**22**	**23**	**24**	**25**	**26**	**27**	28	29	30	31	32	33	34	35	36	37	38						
1	2	3	4	5	**6**	**7**	**8**	**9**	**10**	**11**	**12**	**13**	**14**	**15**	16	17	18	19	20	21	22	23	24	25	26																		
1	2	3	4	5	6	7	8	9	10	11	12	13	14	15	16	17	18	19	20	21	22	**23**	**24**	**25**	**26**	**27**	**28**	**29**	**30**	**31**	**32**	33	34	35	36	37	38	39	40	41	42	43	
1	2	3	4	5	6	**7**	**8**	**9**	**10**	**11**	**12**	**13**	**14**	**15**	**16**	17	18	19	20	21	22	23	24	25	26	27																	
1	2	3	4	5	6	7	8	**9**	**10**	**11**	**12**	**13**	**14**	**15**	**16**	**17**	**18**	19	20	21	22	23	24	25	26	27	28	29															
1	2	3	4	5	6	7	8	9	10	11	12	13	14	**15**	**16**	**17**	**18**	**19**	**20**	**21**	**22**	**23**	**24**	25	26	27	28	29	30	31	32	33	34	35									
1	2	3	4	5	6	7	8	9	**10**	**11**	**12**	**13**	**14**	**15**	**16**	**17**	**18**	**19**	20	21	22	23	24	25	26	27	28	29	30														
1	2	3	4	5	6	7	8	9	10	11	12	13	**14**	**15**	**16**	**17**	**18**	**19**	**20**	**21**	**22**	**23**	24	25	26	27	28	29	30	31	32	33	34										
1	2	3	4	5	6	7	8	9	10	11	12	13	14	15	16	**17**	**18**	**19**	**20**	**21**	**22**	**23**	**24**	**25**	**26**	27	28	29	30	31	32	33	34	35	36	37							

21 Days

Total Length of Cycle	Minus	21 Days	Equals	Last Menstrual/Postmenstrual Infertile Day
44	−	21	=	Day 23
33	−	21	=	Day 12
36	−	21	=	Day 15
38	−	21	=	Day 17

There is a sound basis for relying on the 21-Day Rule. If you look at table 3, you will see that a woman's fertility phase begins three weeks—or 21 days—prior to the onset of menstruation. Thus, it is possible to make a highly reliable calculation of the last day of infertility beyond the fifth day. The technique? Simply subtract 21 from the total length of the cycle.

If you look below the table, you will also see how to apply the 21-Day Rule in the first few cases. All you do is subtract 21 days from the last figure in the column, which is the last day of the cycle. You can also readily cross-check against the diagram to see that the calculation is accurate: The heavy black line is drawn after the last infertile day.

Test yourself by doing the calculations for the rest of the cycles. Check the results of your subtraction against the diagram: The last probable day of infertility is the figure that immediately *precedes* the black line. The results of your subtraction should yield that figure.

Effectiveness of the 21-Day Rule: No controlled study has been done to evaluate the reliability of the 21-Day Rule. But based on wide clinical experience from tens of thousands of couples in the Couple to Couple League, John and Sheila Kippley report in *The Art of Natural Family Planning* that the guideline offers about 99 percent reliability for the menstrual/postmenstrual phase. But the Kippleys emphasize that the 21-Day Rule *is subordinate to the appearance of mucus*.

Still, many couples rely solely on the temperature rise and the so-called 21-Day Rule to determine the total time of infertility after ovulation. If you have records on your previous twelve cycles, you may opt to use this simple means for determining your fertile and infertile phases. If you have complete records for only the past six to eight cycles, you can still apply the 21-Day Rule. Reliability, however, may be less than 99 percent.

Applying the 21-Day Rule: In order to apply the rule reliably, you should have records on the lengths of *your last twelve cycles*. This improves reliability for the woman who occasionally experiences a cycle that is a day or more shorter than usual. Here is how to apply the rule:

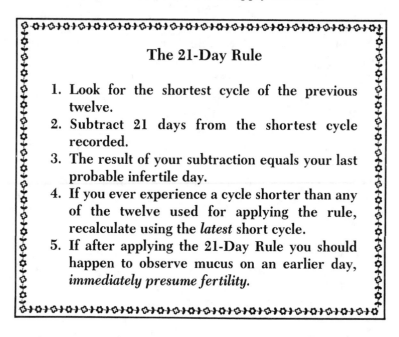

The 21-Day Rule

1. Look for the shortest cycle of the previous twelve.
2. Subtract 21 days from the shortest cycle recorded.
3. The result of your subtraction equals your last probable infertile day.
4. If you ever experience a cycle shorter than any of the twelve used for applying the rule, recalculate using the *latest* short cycle.
5. If after applying the 21-Day Rule you should happen to observe mucus on an earlier day, *immediately presume fertility.*

When the 21-Day Rule Does Not Apply: If you experience more than 16 days of rising and elevated temperatures, it means that for you the time between ovulation and menstruation (technically known as the luteal phase) is very long. You must compensate for this extra length in your calculation. It's easy: Just add one day to the 21-Day Rule for every extra day (beyond 16) of elevated temperatures. Thus, if your chart shows 18 days of higher temperatures, then you must follow a 23-day guideline. (Add an extra day for day 17 and one for day 18.) And, as always, *the unexpected appearance of mucus means that you are fertile.*

As effective as the 21-Day Rule is, most women prefer to learn how to chart mucus changes. So once the "3 and 2 and 6" Guideline is mastered, you are ready for the next learning stage.

Avanti!

7

✿✛✿✛✿✛✿✛✿

How to Chart Your Third and Fourth Cycles

By charting mucus along with temperatures, you can usually extend the infertile phase *beyond* the fifth day of the new menstrual cycle. In addition, the "3 and 2 and 6" Guideline can be relaxed somewhat because you will have two fertility indicators to serve as cross-checks.

Record your mucus each day according to the mucus charting guidelines that follow. One-plus mucus (+) should be marked in the bottom box of the appropriate cycle day. Two-plus mucus (+ +) should be marked in the bottom and middle boxes of the appropriate cycle day. Three-plus mucus (+ + +) is marked in all three boxes, bottom, middle, and top.

One-plus mucus (+):

1	2	3	4	5	6	7
+						

Two-plus mucus (+ +):

8	9	10	11	12	13	14
+						
+						

Three-plus mucus (+ + +):

15	16	17	18	19	20	21
+						
+						
+						

How to Chart Your Mucus

Mark your chart with one plus sign (+) if your mucus has one or more of the early mucus characteristics:

- Consistency of thick paste (yellow or white)
- Tacky
- Opaque (yellow or white)
- Thick

- If placed between thumb and forefinger, tiny peaks are formed when fingers are separated

Mark your chart with two plus signs (+ +) if your mucus has one or more developing mucus characteristics:

- Consistency of creamy hand lotion
- If placed between thumb and forefinger, remains smooth on both fingers when they are separated
- Stretches less than one inch between two fingers

- Cloudy
- Watery
- Milky
- Translucent (colorless or yellowish)
- Sensation of wetness in the genital area ("feels wet")

Mark your chart with three plus signs (+ + +) if your mucus has one or more of the following characteristics:

- Translucent with opaque "threads" running through
- *Feels* wet
- *Feels* slippery
- *Feels* lubricative

- Looks like raw egg white
- Stretches between the fingers an inch or more
- Pink, red, or brown tinge

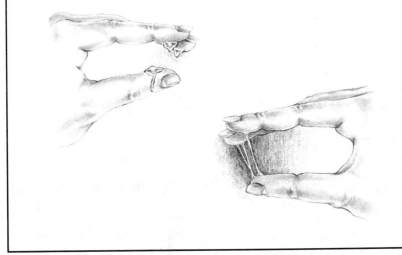

Fertility and the Mucus Sign: Any incidence of mucus means that you are fertile *unless* it is observed during the postovulatory phase of your cycle when your temperature is high. The sustained rise indicates that there is so much progesterone in your body that ovulation can't occur. Thus, you can ignore random appearances of mucus after you have proven infertility according to the Postovulatory Infertility Guideline (which will be explained in a moment).

For now, you must be concerned with evidence of fertility in your menstrual/postmenstrual phase. Here is the guideline to observe along with appropriate exceptions:

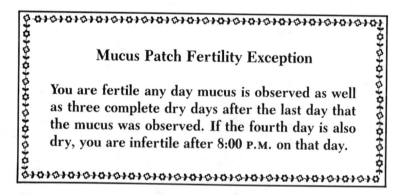

Menstrual/Postmenstrual Infertility Guideline

You are infertile on the evening of all dry days during the menstrual/postmenstrual phase. You must wait until evening because it isn't until then that the complete data about a particular day's dryness or absence of dryness are "in."

There are two exceptions to the Menstrual/Postmenstrual Infertility Guideline: the Mucus Patch Fertility Exception and the Alternate Days Fertility Exception.

Mucus Patch Fertility Exception

You are fertile any day mucus is observed as well as three complete dry days after the last day that the mucus was observed. If the fourth day is also dry, you are infertile after 8:00 P.M. on that day.

For example, if you had one-plus mucus (+) on Tuesday, but are completely dry on Wednesday, Thursday, and Friday, you are fertile from Tuesday straight through and including Friday. If you are dry all day on Saturday, too, you are infertile by that *evening* after 8:00.

Alternate Days Fertility Exception

You are presumed fertile the day and night following any night or morning you had intercourse.

For example, if you had intercourse Sunday night or Monday morning, you are "fertile" all day on Monday, Monday night, and Tuesday. Infertility resumes Tuesday after 8:00 P.M. (when the complete data are "in") if that whole day (Tuesday) was dry.

Seminal Residues and the Cervix Sign: Now, having made the above pronouncement, I will tell you about two exceptions to the second exception!

Experienced women who can distinguish between seminal residues and developing mucus sometimes choose to ignore the Alternate Days Exception during the menstrual/ postmenstrual dry days. Seminal residue has the following characteristics: It will stretch about an inch but breaks down immediately; it may appear as a rubbery, whitish strand, or it may appear foamy and/or will foam slightly if rubbed between the fingers.

Cervical Changes: Once you are experienced with the cervical changes, you can ignore the exception if the information from your cervix clearly indicates that you are infertile.

Mucus Charting Problems: What should you record if you've experienced one-plus (+) in the morning, but by that evening you thought you felt a wet sensation(+ +)?

The guideline is simple: *If you experience two types of mucus within one day, always record the more fertile of the two.**

In the example above, use two plus signs (+ +).

If you are *in doubt* about two mucus types, always assume that you experienced the *more* fertile type. ("If in doubt, you are fertile.") For example, if you aren't sure if your mucus reveals the characteristics of two-plus (+ +) or three-plus (+ + +) translucence, *assume* the latter.

Importance of Sensation: Author Mary Shivanandan reports a case of a woman who ignored the sensation of slipperiness and lubrication on the external genitals because she didn't *see* any mucus. The couple had relations and conceived. Thus, *it is important to be able to distinguish this slippery, lubricative sensation whether or not you can directly see the mucus.*

A slippery, lubricative *sensation* always demands a three-plus (+ + +) indication on your chart. It is the reproductive equivalent of blazing fireworks on the Fourth of July. *This* may be the time that you are about to ovulate! *This* is the time conception is most likely to follow an act of intercourse! If you do not wish to conceive, do not engage in *any* genital-to-genital contact.

Last Day of Mucus: Three-plus mucus (+ + +) is usually the last seen. Sometimes there has been a bit of bleeding when the follicle ruptures. If so, you may detect a red, pink, or brown tinge in the mucus. This is no cause for alarm.

---

*I often refer to mucus as "fertile" or "infertile." In fact, it is neither. As Dr. Rudolf Vollman has noted, the woman is fertile—not the mucus. However, I will keep to the "fertile/infertile mucus" designation because it is a convenient and widely accepted NFP colloquialism.

When the mucus reverts to a less fertile mucus or completely disappears, you can begin to check whether your temperatures "prove" postovulatory infertility.

Of course, you won't be able to tell that any particular day was so-called mucus peak, the last day of most fertile mucus, until after the drying-up process begins—that is, not until a whole day that mucus has reverted to a less "fertile" variety (+ + or + mucus) or dryness has been felt. Otherwise, you have *not* passed the mucus peak and you cannot begin evaluating temperatures for proof of infertility.

Difficulties Establishing the Mucus Peak: Some women never experience any three-plus mucus (+ + +) characteristics: no egg-white mucus; no feelings of wetness, slipperiness, lubrication, etc. If this happens, wait until after the final day of *any* mucus before checking for three high temperature readings.*

Another difficulty: Almost every woman experiences situations of uncertainty. Be prepared for occasions when you think you have passed the last day (because you noticed two or more "drying-up" days in a row), then suddenly you feel slippery, lubricative mucus.

In such a case, disregard your dry-day appearances. Look for the last day of the *new* mucus sign appearance.

Postovulatory Infertility: Once there is a reversion to less fertile mucus, it is time to try to "prove" infertility. This is the guideline devised by Dr. Josef Roetzer to establish postovulatory infertility reliably:

---

*In one study Dr. Roetzer noted that 4.8 percent of the women were without any perceptible mucus[1]. If you discover that you belong to this small group, rely on the 21-Day-Rule at the end of chapter 6 to determine your last menstrual-postmenstrual infertile day.

Postovulatory Infertility Guideline

After mucus peak, wait three high temperature days. Infertility is proven by 8:00 P.M. on the third high temperature day *provided:*

1. All three high temperatures are above all six consecutive low temperatures just before the rise began; and
2. The third high temperature is at least 0.4° above all six lows.

Note: You are no longer looking for three high temperatures *all* at least 0.2° higher than the temperatures in the low set. The new requirement, which relies on two signs, temperature and mucus, demands only that *after* the last day of your most fertile mucus, the peak, all three consecutive high temperatures be above the highest of the consecutive lows. In addition, only the *last* of the three rising temperatures must be at a specific high level—0.4°—above all six of the consecutive lower temperatures.

Once menstruation begins, you are in day 1 of a new cycle and the Menstrual/Postmenstrual Infertility Guidelines apply.

How to Establish a Rise: The first temperature that is above the six immediately preceding it, even if it is only 0.1° above the six, indicates that the rise is beginning.

If Your Last Temperature Isn't High Enough: It may happen to you: Your third high temperature may not achieve the 0.4° high level required. What should you do?

Easy. In exchange for forgetting about the 0.4° temperature height requirement, all you have to do is wait for one *more* high temperature day. So you will look for four—not three—days in which all the temperatures are above all six of the consecutive lower temperatures.

Special Information for Women with Short Cycles: If you ever experience cycles 26 days or shorter, don't be surprised if you have to wait until the postovulatory phase before you can identify infertile days. There may be few or no infertile days during the menstrual/postmenstrual phase because the onset of mucus may coincide with the end of the bleeding.

Also be aware that coitus during the very last days of a prolonged (i.e., longer than five days) menstrual bleeding may cause conception. The possibility is slight, but does exist.

To refresh your memory on the above points, reread the section "Infertility in the New Cycle" in chapter 3.

Intercourse During Menstruation: There is no physical reason for a couple to avoid intercourse during the menses. Of course, some couples find it unaesthetic and prefer to wait. However, other couples are quite indifferent to the bleeding. Still, there are some matters to keep in mind if you have intercourse during menstruation.

A woman who is at risk for pelvic inflammatory disease (PID) should be aware that menstrual blood is an excellent culture medium for PID-causing bacteria. As a result, PID can be more readily introduced into the reproductive tract if a couple has sexual relations during the time of menstrual bleeding.

As for intercourse itself, menstrual blood is generally a good lubricant. Nevertheless, use of tampons may actually dry out the vagina. If this happens to you, there is an easy remedy: Use a lubricant.

If a woman doesn't have an orgasm during lovemaking, she may experience symptoms of cramping and discomfort. These symptoms are caused by increased pelvic congestion. But there is a flip side to this: Orgasm often *decreases* pelvic congestion. As a result, coitus helps some women to feel more comfortable during the menstrual days.

Continuing Your Charting

During the next two cycles record the mucus changes and the waking temperatures every day, beginning with the first day of your menstrual period (day 1). Later it will be possible to cut back on days of temperature-taking, but don't do this until you have recorded these two complete cycles.

Tips for the Following Charts: You can make these assumptions for all the charts that follow:

- All charts are preceded by a charted cycle in which a previous temperature rise was recorded. Thus, bleedings are menstrual and the appropriate Menstrual/Postmenstrual Guidelines apply, including infertility through day 5.
- Infertility always begins at 8:00 P.M. on the day it is "proved."
- Days of intercourse are recorded by circling the cycle day when coitus occurred.

Of course, frequency of lovemaking is a private matter. Should you ever wish to seek NFP guidance or help, only two intercourse days need be shown: Your *last* in the menstrual/postmenstrual phase and your *first* in the ovulatory or postovulatory phase.

Other Fertility Observations: During these two cycles you can begin checking your cervix each morning to note the changes. Do not try to record any cervical changes; just see if you can begin to feel them. Refer to chapter 8 for details.

Some couples don't wish to learn the cervical indicators, since they are assured of effectiveness by monitoring the mucus sign and the temperature rise sign. Still, some NFP instructors feel that it is a good idea to try to see if you can notice the changes. The information could be helpful if you are in an atypical or unusual fertility situation, such as after childbirth or during the premenopause, or if you are highly irregular. But if you don't want to learn them, rest assured that the temperature and mucus signs will give you highly effective fertility control without any reliance on the cervix whatsoever.

Chart No. 4—Typical Mucus and Temperature: The five days of menstruation are indicated by the "M" in the mucus box section. Monica is infertile until the onset of mucus on day 16.

Monica experiences the last day of lubricative, stretchy mucus (+ + +), the peak, on day 23. On day 24 she begins evaluating her temperatures to "prove" postovulatory infertility. Here are the three easy steps she followed:

1. She identified day 23 as the first day of the rise ("one temperature higher than the preceding six").

2. Monica numbered in reverse her six consecutive low temperatures before the rise, then drew a line along the site of the highest of the six (97.6°).

3. On day 24, the day after the mucus peak, Monica begins circling the three high temperatures. The third one is more than 0.4° above all six of the low temperatures before the rise.

Thus, Monica proves infertility on day 26. (Note: The slight temperature dip on day 32 and mucus on day 33 are ignored because infertility has already been proved.)

Notice that according to the 1 to 16 count-back, Monica ovulated sometime between days 20 and 24.

CHART NO. 4
Typical Mucus and Temperature

PERSONAL FERTILITY CHART

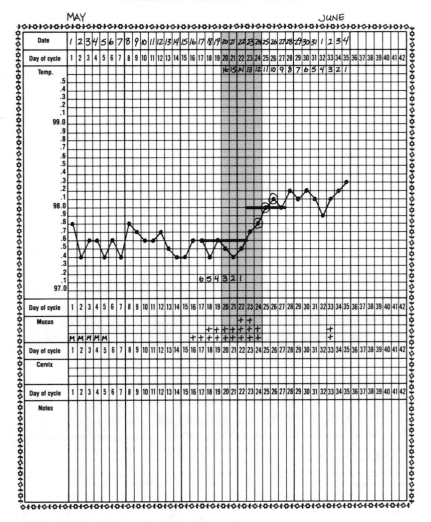

Recorded cycle number: **13**
Shortest previous cycle: **34** days
Number of days in this cycle: **35** days

Chart No. 5—No 0.4° Higher Temperature: Katie presumes fertility on day 10 and day 14 because intercourse occurred the previous evenings. (Also note that on days 6–8 interrupted sleep causes slightly elevated temperatures.) Mucus is observed on day 15 signaling the onset of the ovulatory phase.

Starting on day 21, after the mucus peak, Katie begins evaluating her signs to determine infertility.

1. Katie identifies the first day of the rise ("one temperature higher than the preceding six") on day 20.

2. The six consecutive low temperatures before the rise are numbered in reverse and Katie draws a line along the site of the highest, at 97.5°.

3. Starting on day 21, Katie circles three high temperatures above the first line, but the third temperature is not 0.4° above all six lows. Katie must wait for one more high temperature day before she "proves" infertility on day 24.

Look at the 1 to 16 count-back: Katie must have ovulated sometime between days 20 and 23 because day 24 falls within the ovulatory range. She had relations but didn't conceive. See how important it is to wait for a *fourth* confirming temperature?

CHART NO. 5
No 0.4° Higher Temperature on Third Day

PERSONAL FERTILITY CHART

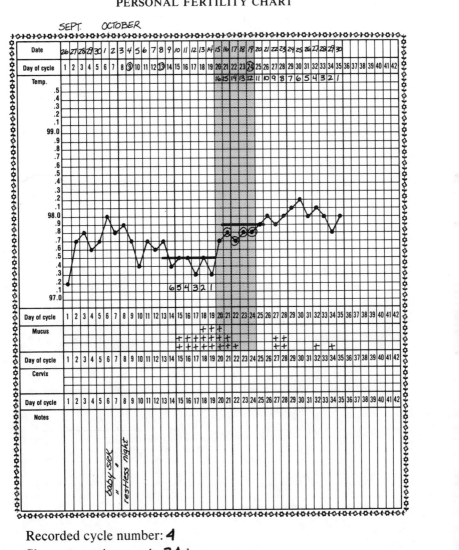

Recorded cycle number: **4**
Shortest previous cycle: **34** days
Number of days in this cycle: **35** days

Chart No. 6—Delayed Ovulation: Notice that on this chart Carol's most fertile mucus stops not once, not twice, but *three* times, on days 12, 15, and 22 (see arrows). Carol is experiencing the fits and starts of a delayed ovulation and has three mucus peaks.

Each time her most fertile mucus stops, she begins evaluating the temperatures to see if she can determine the beginning of a rise and the onset of her postovulatory infertile time. No luck the first two times, but after day 22 matters brighten considerably.

First of all, day 22 itself is not only the last day of Carol's most fertile mucus but also the first day that a temperature is recorded that is higher than the preceding six lows.

Carol numbers the six low temperatures in reverse and looks for the high temperatures after the (third) mucus peak. The highs start on day 24, but Carol must wait for a fourth temperature because her third one isn't 0.4° above the highest of the six lows.

According to the 1 to 16 count-back, Carol ovulated sometime between days 21 and 25. Thus, her calculation of day 27 infertility allows a few days' margin for error.

CHART NO. 6
Delayed Ovulation

PERSONAL FERTILITY CHART

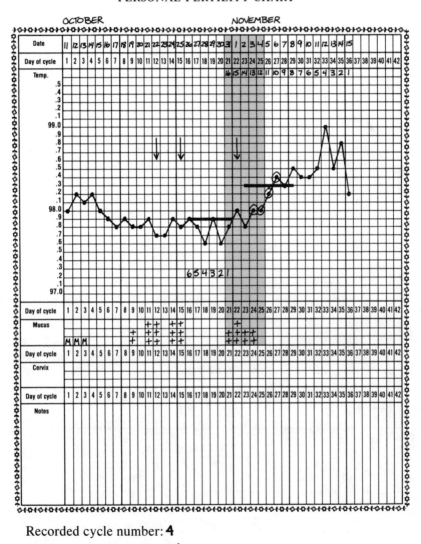

Recorded cycle number: **4**

Shortest previous cycle: **34** days

Number of days in this cycle: **36** days

Chart No. 7—Fertile Mucus During Temperature Rise: Louise's chart demonstrates the importance of waiting until *after* the mucus peak before the temperatures can be evaluated to prove infertility.

Louise is fertile on days 6, 8, and 10 after previous-night intercourses. (See Alternate Days Fertility Exception, earlier in this chapter.)

The ovulatory phase begins with the onset of mucus on day 13. Notice that Louise's temperature rise begins on day 16 and continues through days 17 and 18, but Louise waits until day 19, after her most fertile-type mucus (+ + +) has stopped, before she begins evaluating her temperatures.

All three of the temperatures starting on day 19 are high temperatures. The day 21 temperature is 0.4° above the highest of the six lows. Thus, Louise proves infertility on that day.

The 1 to 16 count-back shows that Louise ovulated sometime between days 16 and 20.

As always, random appearances of mucus after postovulatory infertility is proved can be ignored.

CHART NO. 7
Fertile Mucus During Temperature Rise

PERSONAL FERTILITY CHART

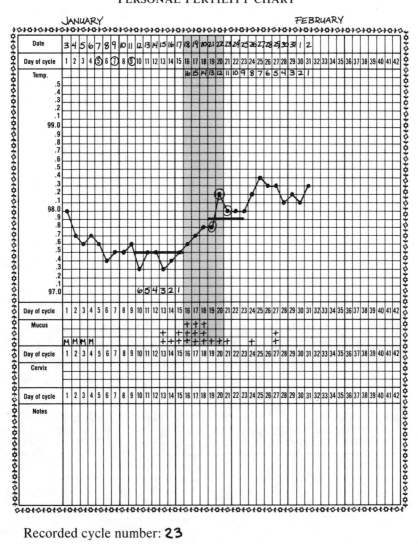

Recorded cycle number: **23**
Shortest previous cycle: **28** days
Number of days in this cycle: **31** days

Chart No. 8—Less Fertile Mucus: Bridget doesn't have mucus with three-plus (+ + +) characteristics. Her most fertile mucus type is milky and cloudy in appearance and has very little "stretch." It is two-plus mucus (+ +).

This type of situation is discussed earlier in this chapter, in "Difficulties Establishing the Mucus Peak." Bridget must wait until *all* mucus has stopped before she can begin evaluating her temperatures. Thus, Bridget waits until day 18, her first "dry" day, to start circling her temperatures.

Something else crops up in Bridget's chart: Her third high temperature is not 0.4° higher than any of the low temperatures just before the rise began. Is this a problem? Not at all.

As mentioned earlier in this chapter, when the third temperature isn't high enough, it is necessary to wait for one more high temperature. This fourth temperature doesn't have to be 0.4° higher than any of the lows, but it must be a *high* temperature. Bridget's fourth temperature meets this requirement. Thus, Bridget proves infertility on day 21.

The 1 to 16 count-back shows that ovulation occurred sometime between days 14 and 18.

CHART NO. 8
Less Fertile Mucus

PERSONAL FERTILITY CHART

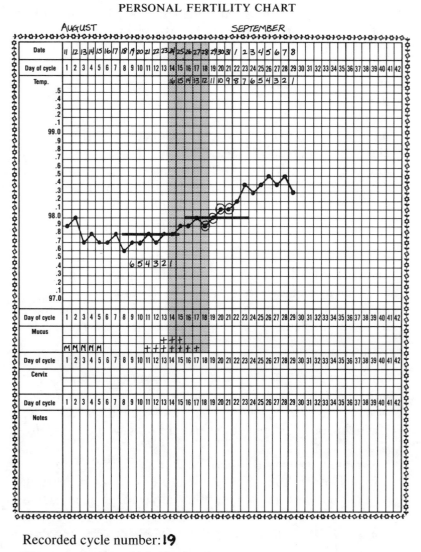

Recorded cycle number: **19**

Shortest previous cycle: **27** days

Number of days in this cycle: **29** days

When Your Chart Doesn't Fit the Guidelines

Speaking at the International Symposium on Natural Family Planning conducted at the Human Life Center at St. John's University in Collegeville, Minnesota, in June 1977, Dr. Roetzer made a cautionary comment about his guideline: "[The guideline] is sufficient for almost all cases; there are only a few cases where you cannot apply this rule; and there is *no* rule which is appropriate for *all* cases."

Dr. Roetzer's cautionary comment is important to remember, since every couple occasionally experiences cycles that either don't meet the guidelines or are hard to interpret. In such situations, of course, the "If in doubt, you are fertile" rule is applicable. If it is important to avoid pregnancy, defer intercourse until infertility can definitely be proved.

Of course, this is where experience will stand you in good stead. There may be times when you will have to discuss the guidelines, try to understand what has gone on, and then make a determination as to whether or not you are fertile or infertile at a particular time. Some of the most frequent problems are discussed in the next few pages.

What to Do About Fevers: Disregard any temperature caused by fever. *Be especially alert to very mild fevers. Flu or a cold may cause only a slight rise of two- or three-tenths of a degree.* You could mistake these temperatures for the beginning of a rise, but such temperatures would be *a false rise.*

Do *not* use your BBT thermometer if you know you have a high temperature. The temperature will not accurately reflect your fertility or infertility anyway. Instead, use a regular fever thermometer and note on the chart that you are sick. *Do not rely on higher temperatures that are recorded when you are sick.*

Consider yourself fertile until any possible cold, flu, or

fever temperature has been gone for three full days. Then after the three days have passed, evaluate your chart very carefully to check that all the other infertility signs are present. If they are still present the *following* day—that is, the fourth day—then you can presume infertility after 8:00 P.M.

Unusually High Temperatures: Very high temperatures in the menstrual/postmenstrual phase can present a different problem. Determining the highest of your lowest six consecutive temperatures would be difficult if one temperature towers way above the rest in the set. Should this happen, you would be forced to draw a line that is so high none of the later postovulatory high temperatures could satisfy the requirement to prove infertility.

What do you do?

First, *you can always completely discount ONE unexpected high temperature in the menstrual/postmenstrual phase.* Such unexpected highs occur from time to time and can be safely ignored if they appear among a cluster of five other low temperatures. Thus, *cancel* the unexpected high temperature in your calculations.

Still, any sudden temperature rise of 0.5° or more in one day is suspect. As I have said, it can be ignored if it appears among the six lowest menstrual/postmenstrual temperatures. *But a sudden high temperature can never be ignored if it is one of the three high postovulatory temperatures. You must wait for one more (i.e., a fourth) confirmatory high temperature.*

Chart No. 9—Unusually High Temperature: Theresa is infertile for the first 11 days of her cycle. Fertility begins on day 12 when she observes tacky mucus (+).

On day 15 Theresa records an unusually high temperature. She cancels it. A few days later her slippery, egg-white mucus (+ + +) has stopped and the beginning of a temperature rise is indicated ("one temperature higher than the previous six").

Theresa circles three higher temperatures after the mucus peak. In this chart all three happen to be at least 0.4° higher than the highest of the preceding six low temperatures. What a splendid temperature rise confirmation!

Thus, Theresa proves infertility by day 22. The 1 to 16 count-back shows that she ovulated sometime between day 17 and day 21.

CHART NO. 9
Unusually High Temperature

PERSONAL FERTILITY CHART

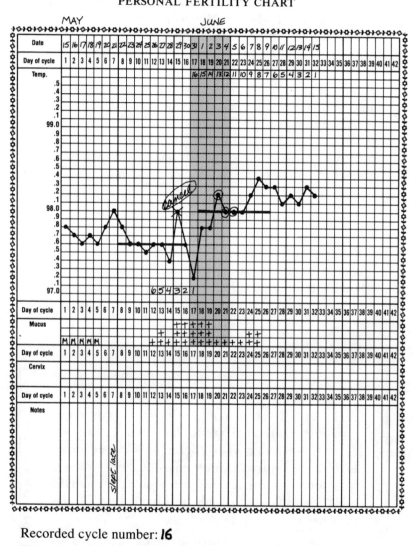

Recorded cycle number: **16**

Shortest previous cycle: **31** days

Number of days in this cycle: **32** days

Chart No. 10—Double Jeopardy: As you can see, Susan's chart shows two unusually high temperatures on days 13 and 14. A lot of instructors call those two highs the weekend syndrome! Maybe so. Nevertheless, Susan still has to wait until day 21 to prove infertility.

Double Jeopardy: What if you have *two* unexpected high temperatures in what you were hoping could be your set of six low temperatures? This can be tricky. With certain restrictions (see the Double Jeopardy Guideline below) you can disregard two unusually high temperatures *if* there are extraneous factors that explain them. The most common of these factors are:

- Cold or flu symptoms
- Sleeping unusually late
- Experiencing an unaccustomed chill or heat (After one couple began using an electric blanket, the woman's waking temperature rose for several consecutive days.)
- Unusual alcohol consumption the previous night

DOUBLE JEOPARDY GUIDELINE

If you discount temperatures in the menstrual/postmenstrual phase for valid extraneous reasons, consider yourself fertile for one extra high temperature day in the postovulatory phase. The temperature on this extra day (the fourth) must be at least 0.4° above the highest of the presumed lows.

CHART NO. 10
Double Jeopardy

PERSONAL FERTILITY CHART

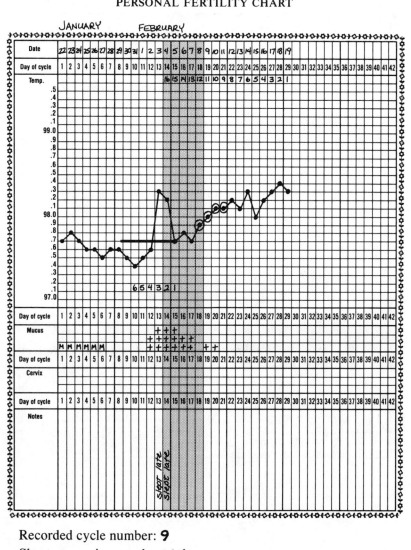

Recorded cycle number: **9**
Shortest previous cycle: **26** days
Number of days in this cycle: **29** days

Chart No. 11—Temperature Dip Pattern: Here a rising trend is recorded after the mucus peak. However, the third temperature after cessation of Annette's most fertile mucus dips *below* the highest of the six temperatures before the rise.

This kind of temperature-dip pattern shows up cycle after cycle in a few women. It is a frequent pattern for Annette, who takes it in stride.

Annette knows that one low temperature among the three postmucus peak temperatures can be ignored, but that the last temperature—the fourth—must be at least 0.4° above the highest of the six lowest temperatures just before the rise begins. (Special note: If the fourth temperature doesn't reach this level, wait for a fifth-day high temperature. The fifth high temperature need only be a *high* temperature, not specifically 0.4° higher than the highest of the six lows.)

In this case Annette ignores the low temperature on day 18 and proves infertility on day 19. She had intercourse that evening after 8:00 P.M.

Notice the retrospective count-back: Annette ovulated sometime between days 15 and 18. If she had not waited the extra day, she might have conceived from a possible day 18 ovulation.

CHART NO. 11
Temperature Dip Pattern

PERSONAL FERTILITY CHART

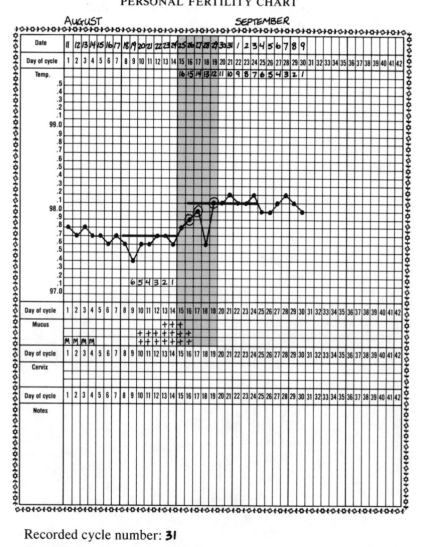

Recorded cycle number: **31**
Shortest previous cycle: **28** days
Number of days in this cycle: **30** days

Do-It-Yourself Charts

So far you have looked at completed charts. It is easy to make determinations about fertility and infertility when all the information is laid out so nicely. But in real life we have to make *day-by-day* decisions about fertility.

This is why I'm giving you information listing the temperature and mucus signs for each cycle day for charting three practice cycles. Using copies of the Personal Fertility Chart at the back of the book, fill in the temperatures by placing a dot in the middle of the line of the square under the day right across from the temperature and then connect your lines. Fill in the mucus boxes with the appropriate number of plus signs.

As you place your dot and plus signs for each day, try to determine whether *that* day is fertile or infertile. When the chart is complete, determine:

1. The menstrual/postmenstrual infertile days
2. The fertile days
3. The first postovulatory infertile day

("Fertility puzzle" answers can be found after the third practice cycle along with commentary to explain the answer. Don't peek until you have figured out each chart on your own!)

Information for Practice Cycle No. 1

Day 1: Menstruation (M) following a sustained temperature rise in previous cycle. 98.1°

Day 2: Menstruation. 98.0°

Day 3: Menstruation. 97.8°

Day 4: Menstruation. 97.8°

Day 5: Menstruation. 97.7°

Day 6: Dry. 97.6°

Day 7: Wet sensation. 97.4°

Day 8: Tacky mucus. 97.5°

Day 9: Tacky mucus. 97.5°

Day 10: Wet sensation. 97.4°

Day 11: Lubricative sensation. 97.6°

Day 12: Raw-egg-white mucus. 98.0°

Day 13: Tacky mucus. 97.8°

Day 14: Tacky mucus. 98.0°

Day 15: Tacky, yellow mucus. 98.6°

Day 16: Tacky, yellow mucus. 98.3°

Day 17: Wet sensation. 98.4°

Day 18: Dry. 98.2°

Day 19: Dry. 98.4°

Day 20: Dry. 98.4°

Day 21: Dry. 98.5°

Day 22: Dry. 98.3°

Day 23: Dry. 98.5°

Day 24: Dry. 98.4°

Day 25: Dry. 98.4°

Day 26: Dry. 98.3°

Day 27: Dry. 98.3°

Information for Practice Cycle No. 2

Day 1: Menstruation (M) following a sustained temperature rise in previous cycle. 97.8°

Day 2: Menstruation. 97.7°

Day 3: Menstruation. 97.8°

Day 4: Menstruation. 97.6°

Day 5: Menstruation. 97.8°

Day 6: Dry. 98.0°

Day 7: Dry. 97.8°

Day 8: Dry. 97.8°

Day 9: Dry. 97.7°

Day 10: Dry. 97.4°

Day 11: Dry. 97.7°

Day 12: Dry. 97.6°

Day 13: Dry. 97.7°

Day 14: Dry. 97.4°

Day 15: Dry. 97.5°

Day 16: Cloudy mucus. 97.5°

Day 17: Translucent mucus. 97.3°

Day 18: Raw-egg-white mucus. 97.5°

Day 19: Raw-egg-white mucus. 97.3°

Day 20: Dry. 97.7°

Day 21: Dry. 98.2°

Day 22: Dry. 98.2°

Day 23: Dry. 98.3°

Day 24: Dry. 98.4°

Day 25: Dry. 98.3°

Day 26: Dry. 98.5°

Day 27: Dry. 98.5°

Day 28: Dry. 98.3°

Day 29: Dry. 98.4°

Day 30: Dry. 98.5°

Day 31: Dry. 98.4°

Day 32: Dry. 98.4°

Day 33: Dry. 98.3°

Day 34: Dry. 98.3°

Information for Practice Cycle No. 3

Day 1: Menstruation following sustained temperature rise in previous cycle. 98.6°

Day 2: Menstruation. 98.1°

Day 3: Menstruation. 97.7°

Day 4: Menstruation. 98.0°

Day 5: Menstruation. 97.8°

Day 6: Dry. 97.4°

Day 7: Dry. 97.2°

Day 8: Dry. 97.5°

Day 9: Wet sensation. 97.6°

Day 10: Tacky, yellow mucus. 97.3°

Day 11: Tacky, yellow mucus. 97.3°

Day 12: Tacky, yellow mucus. 97.3°

Day 13: Slippery sensation. 97.4°

Day 14: Slippery sensation. 97.6°

Day 15: Slippery sensation. 97.8°

Day 16: Slippery sensation. 97.5°

Day 17: Raw-egg-white mucus. 98.1°

Day 18: Raw-egg-white mucus. 97.9°

Day 19: Dry. 98.0°

Day 20: Dry. 98.1°

Day 21: Dry. 98.0°

Day 22: Dry. 98.2°

Day 23: Dry. 98.1°

Day 24: Dry. 98.0°

Day 25: Dry. 98.0°

Day 26: Dry. 97.8°

Day 27: Dry. 98.0°

Practice Cycle No. 1: The fertile/infertile days are:

Infertile: Through day 6
Fertile: Day 7 through day 14
Infertile: 8:00 P.M., day 15

Miriam's cycle follows a temperature rise in the previous cycle. Thus, infertility lasts through the first 5 days as well as day 6, which is a dry day. Mucus is noted on day 7 and signals the onset of the fertile phase. The last day of the most fertile mucus, the peak, occurs on day 12.

Postovulatory infertility is determined according to the guideline as follows:

1. The first day of Miriam's rise is identified on day 12 ("one temperature higher than the preceding six").
2. The six consecutive low temperatures occur on days 6, 7, 8, 9, 10, and 11. 97.6° is the highest temperature of the six.
3. Miriam records three high temperatures above all six consecutive low temperatures on days 13, 14, and 15. The temperature on day 15 meets the requirement that it be 0.4° higher than any of the six lows.

Practice Cycle No. 2: The fertile/infertile days are:

Infertile: Day 1 through day 15
Fertile: Day 16 through day 21
Infertile: 8:00 P.M., day 22

This chart is unusual because Maureen is fertile only 7 days out of 34. Most couples experience *at least* 9 to 10 days of fertility.

No mucus appears for the first 15 days. Mucus is observed for the first time on day 16. The most fertile mucus stops on day 19.

Infertility is determined according to the Postovulatory Infertility Guideline as follows:

1. The rise is identified on day 20 ("one temperature higher than the preceding six").
2. The six consecutive lows occur on days 14 through 19 and the highest is 97.5° (which occurs three times).
3. The day after the mucus peak (day 20) is the first of the three high temperature days. The last, day 22, is 0.4° above the highest of the six lows before the rise began.

Practice Cycle No. 3: The fertile/infertile days are:

Infertile: Through day 8
Fertile: Day 9 through day 20
Infertile: 8:00 P.M., day 21

Fertility begins on day 9 when Patricia detects a sensation of wetness in the genital area. Mucus continues through day 18, the last day of her most fertile mucus, the peak. The following day Pat is dry, and the dryness continues through the rest of the cycle. Here is how she determines postovulatory infertility according to the guideline:

1. The temperature rise is identified on day 15 ("one temperature higher than the preceding six").
2. Pat's six consecutive low temperatures are numbered in reverse (days 9 through 14) with a line drawn above the highest of the six (97.6°).
3. The day after her mucus peak (day 19), Pat begins circling her three high temperatures. The last, on day 21, is 0.4° above all six of the low temperatures before the rise.

Some Final Words About Temperatures

By the time you have recorded two complete cycles on your own, you may be ready to reduce temperature-taking to two weeks or less out of your cycle. To do this, you must take your waking temperature long enough to get six consecutive low temperatures to use as a base.

Cutting Back on Temperature-Taking: Many women begin taking the waking temperature after mucus is noticed. For example, if mucus is felt or observed anytime on Tuesday, temperature-taking begins Wednesday morning.

Temperature-taking continues until the third high waking temperature is recorded, provided it is 0.4° above the highest of the six consecutive lowest temperatures before the rise. If the third high waking temperature *doesn't* meet the "0.4° above" test, then waking temperatures must be taken on succeeding mornings until the requirement is satisfied. Temperature-taking can then cease, to be resumed when mucus is felt and/or observed in the *succeeding* cycle.

Short Cycles: Waiting until mucus develops before you start taking the waking temperature can be a problem if you have cycles shorter than 27 days. You may not be able to accumulate enough temperatures to establish six lows. Solution? Begin taking your waking temperature the fourth or fifth day of the cycle.

Forgetting to Take Temperatures: You may miss one day or even several days in a row of temperature-taking. Don't be discouraged; missing a day (or a few) happens to everyone and is considerably less of a problem than missing one or more contraceptive pills!

It is better not to omit temperatures, but if it happens, just leave the square (or squares) blank. In other words, do *not* draw a connecting line. Connecting lines are drawn only between *consecutive* temperatures.

Continue temperature-taking as soon as possible. *However, try not to forget during your first six learning cycles.* In this initial period be very careful to record all information about your fertility and infertility. If you are careful in the beginning, you will gain enough experience to judge the approximate site of the low and and high temperature phases from only a few readings. This experience will stand you in good stead if you later forget to take your temperature in a different cycle. However, observe this one cautionary guideline: *If you forget to take your temperature for a number of days, take a fourth temperature before considering yourself infertile.*

For example, with experience you may notice that your low temperatures usually hover around 97.5° to 97.7°. In contrast, your high temperature phase is usually about 98.2° to 98.5°. If you miss taking your temperature for a week but are sure that you have passed your mucus peak, begin temperature-taking right away. If your thermometer registers 98.4°, 98.3°, 98.5°, and 98.4° on four successive days, you may assume you are infertile provided there are no disturbing factors that might cause a higher temperature reading.

Note: Do not make this assumption concerning postovulatory infertility unless you have at least six cycles' experience with charting. You must have this experience before you can take shortcuts.

Different Waking Times: You may be up and down during the night—sick children, new baby, whatever—and not be able to take your temperature at a regular time. This is not ideal, but can be accommodated.

The best thing to do is to try to take your temperature at more or less the same time and when you have had your longest stretch of uninterrupted sleep. Even if this turns out to be a short stretch between midnight and 3:00 or 4:00 A.M. (only three or four hours of sleep), take your temperature then.

If for some reason you only get an hour or two of sleep, take your temperature and make note of the disturbance. Keep one thing in mind: *Some* kind of a record is better than *no* kind of a record!

Unplanned Pregnancy

Only complete abstinence offers 100 percent assurance that pregnancy won't occur. Selective abstinence based on the correct identification of the fertile times offers 99.2 percent reliability. The combination Pill and surgical sterilization can also offer this reliability, but with health risks.

Should you become pregnant following Dr. Roetzer's guidelines, he would like the opportunity to study your charts. He asks, however, that your pregnancy be *truly unexplained.* That is, that you have kept to the guidelines, refraining from all fertile-time sexual contact, including genital-to-genital (penis to vulva) contact without penetration, and that you have never had intercourse using any type of contraceptive.

Please send *all* your original charts beginning with your *first* day of charting. Be sure that your name is on a covering letter and include information on where you learned about NFP (mention this book by name) as well as information on how you take your temperature (orally, rectally, vaginally).

Send the material, with your return address, to:

> Dr. Josef Roetzer
> Vorstadt 6
> A-4840 Voecklabruck
> Austria

Please allow eight to twelve weeks for reply.

8

✧⊁✧⊁✧⊁✧

Charting
for the Rest of
Your Fertile Years

By monitoring mucus and temperature changes alone, you will have the security of knowing when you are fertile and when you are not fertile *for the rest of your fertile years.* From now on you can be completely independent of any-*one* or any*thing* when you plan your family.

If you have also opted to examine your cervix each day, it is now time to learn a way to make an appropriate record of cervical changes.

Reliability of the Cervical Sign: Before beginning, I want to remind you that there are no effectiveness studies on the reliability of the cervical sign. Many women find the sign to be very helpful; others do not.

The cervical sign is of greatest use for women who either have very scanty mucus (which is sometimes the case for premenopausal women) or experience a continuous mucus discharge (as sometimes happens to breast-feeding mothers). It is also useful during periods of stress or illness when there may be a delayed ovulation or a fever which throws off the temperature sign. In such cases the daily cervical check is of particular value: Once the cervix begins to open, soften, and rise, you will have additional evidence of the renewed beginning of a possible ovulatory phase.

Learning the Cervical Changes: Recognizing the cervical changes requires no more internal self-inspection than you may have used when you checked your IUD string or the placement of your diaphragm if you used those artificial methods. If your hands are clean and your nails reasonably well trimmed, you will not hurt yourself or cause any tearing or bleeding.

There is only one matter to bear in mind: Check your cervix at a time *apart* from your regular bowel elimination. A full bowel can distort the interpretation of the cervix as either "low," "rising," or "high." So check an hour or so after elimination.

Many women find that the easiest way to check the cervix is while sitting on the toilet. Others stand with one foot on the floor and the other raised on the toilet seat, the edge of the bathtub, or on a stool.

If you use tampons, insert your finger in the same way. Aim your fingers in the general direction of your chin.

If the vagina is too dry to accept a finger, use water for wetting. *Don't* use K-Y jelly or a similar product; lubricants may make it difficult to distinguish slippery mucus accurately.

If water is necessary because of excessive dryness, this is probably an indication that you are infertile.

Best Time to Learn: Dr. Roetzer reports that it is best to learn the cervical sign toward the end of the fertile time, after the mucus peak. "Women are always astonished at how quickly the cervix becomes firm (like the cartilage in the tip of the nose) and tightly closed, after having been soft

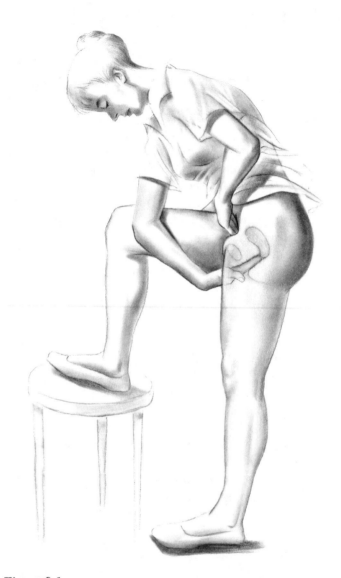

Figure 8.1
The standing position for checking the cervix is most effective when you gently push against your stomach with one hand. This makes it easier for your finger to make contact with your cervix. An alternative position favored by many women is seated on the toilet with the upper body bent slightly forward.

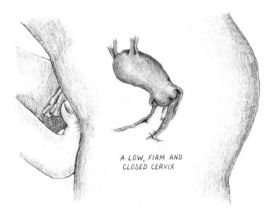

A LOW, FIRM AND
CLOSED CERVIX

Figure 8.2

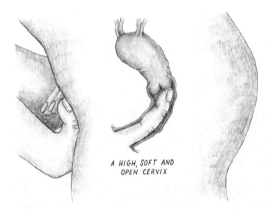

A HIGH, SOFT AND
OPEN CERVIX

Figure 8.3

When you are infertile, your finger can easily touch your cervix, which is low in the vagina. The *os* ("mouth") is also closed, and the cervix feels firm to the touch. As you enter your fertile phase, your cervix will rise progressively higher in the vagina and will also open and soften to your touch. Sometimes during the fertile time the cervix rises so high that it becomes impossible to reach. If you can't reach your cervix, you are fertile!

and open," he reports.[1] So once your mucus sign indicates that you are in the fertile phase, begin checking your cervix. This will give you an opportunity to feel all the changes within a matter of days.

You will be looking for three changes: position of the cervix; the cervical opening; the texture of the cervix.

The illustrations (figures 8.1, 8.2, and 8.3) are a good guide to help you learn how to check the changing position of the cervix.

The cervical opening feels different depending on whether or not you have delivered a child vaginally. The opening is dimplelike if you haven't. After a vaginal delivery, the cervical opening is more like a slit. You can compare the differences by looking at figure 8.4.

Record the changes according to the guidelines listed in the box that follows, entitled "Charting the Cervical Changes."

Cervical Charting Problems: What should you record if you have felt that the cervix has one plus sign (+) characteristics in the morning (it is low, firm, and closed), but by the evening it appears to have two plus sign (+ +) characteristics (say, you detect a slight rise)?

The guideline is similar to the mucus sign guideline: *If you experience a cervical change within a single day, record the more fertile change of the two.*

In the example you would record two plus signs (+ +).

If you are in doubt about whether your cervix reflects two plus sign characteristics (+ +) or three (+ + +), always assume the more fertile. ("If in doubt, you are fertile.")

Continuous Mucus and Cervical Changes: If you are learning the cervical changes because you experience a continuous mucus discharge, you must monitor the mucus

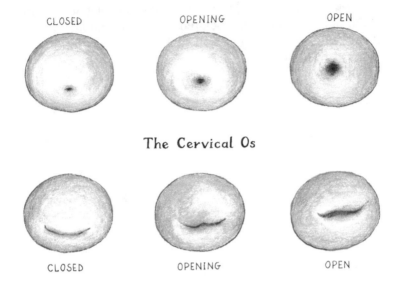

The Cervical Os

Figure 8.4

The top row shows the dimplelike appearance of your cervix if you have not delivered a child vaginally. The bottom row shows its slitlike appearance if you have had a vaginal delivery. The cervices on the extreme left indicate infertility because they are closed; those on the extreme right are open and so indicate fertility.

carefully: Any fluctuation in the mucus type may indicate the onset of fertility. Likewise if there is any change in the cervix. (But since you are just learning the cervical changes, it is safer to presume that the cervical change may not be noticed at first.) Generally, as long as the continuing mucus *doesn't* change and remains consistent (though constant), the couple can presume infertility. *However, this is a situation that is best dealt with under the guidance of an experienced teacher.*

Another matter: If there is any unpleasant odor or any unfamiliar discharge associated with continuous mucus, check with your doctor. You may have an infection that requires treatment.

Charting the Cervical Changes

Mark your chart with one plus sign (+) if your cervix has all three of the following characteristics:

- low
- closed
- firm (feels like the cartilage in your nose tip)

Mark your chart with two plus signs (+ +) if your cervix has any *one* of the following characteristics:

- rising *or* descending as compared to the previous day
- opening *or* closing as compared to the previous day
- tilted at a slightly different angle as compared to the previous day
- softening *or* hardening as compared to the previous day

Mark your chart with three plus signs (+ + +) if your cervix has any *one* of the following characteristics:

- high, even unreachable
- open
- soft (feels yielding, like your lip)

Chart No. 12—Delayed Ovulation: You have actually seen this chart before. It is from the last chapter (chart no. 6), and it shows the fits and starts of Carol's delayed ovulation.

Of course, the last time you looked at the chart, it was without the cervical changes. On this chart you can see how the cervix changes almost in lockstep with the mucus. By checking both signs, Carol had double confirmation of her body's renewed attempts to ovulate on three separate occasions. Carol's ovulatory delays were caused by severe stress that she was undergoing at the time. Curiously, stress almost never "brings on" an ovulation. It almost invariably delays it.

Mindy had a chart that looked something like Carol's. Not only was the family in the throes of an interstate move, but while the movers were at work, Mindy's six-year-old had an accident and fractured his leg. So in the middle of all of *that,* the couple dashed to the hospital with their by-then hysterical son. Later in reviewing her chart, Mindy was astonished to notice how completely her body had "translated" all the stress.

Several women have told me that while they were in school every menstruation due around exam time was invariably delayed. In reality the pre-exam stress had delayed every *ovulation,* so naturally, the subsequent menstruations came later than expected.

Every woman reacts differently—and sometimes not at all—to different stresses. Charting will help you to learn your special stress points.

CHART NO. 12
Delayed Ovulation

PERSONAL FERTILITY CHART

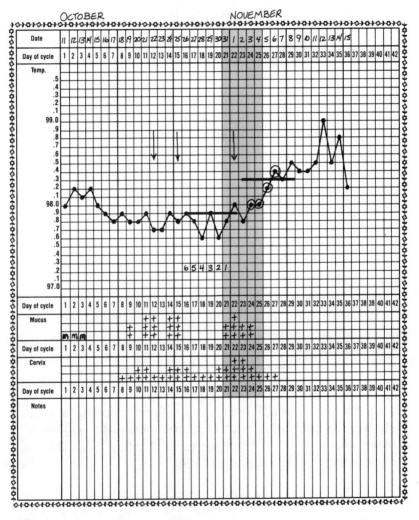

Recorded cycle number: **4**

Shortest previous cycle: **34** days

Number of days in this cycle: **36** days

9

❀❁❀❁❀❁❀

Special Situations

Various circumstances can affect your body, causing normal fluctuations in your fertility signs. Seven situations in which altered fertility patterns are frequently observed are:

- Coming off the Pill
- "Cycles" without ovulation (anovulatory and delayed cycles)
- Miscarriage
- Postpartum, including partial breast-feeding
- The premenopause
- Stress
- Change in diet and/or exercise

These special situations require extra attention and vigilance because your body is responding to circumstances that aren't present in your ordinary cycles. But *do* consult your doctor if you have unexplained bleeding, foul-smelling discharges, or any sign of irritation.

Coming off the Pill

Women who have been on the Pill may discover that their cycles take a long time to return to normal. For a small percentage ovulation may be delayed for months, even for years. A tiny handful of women are left permanently sterile because of permanent suppression of the ovarian function. Still, most women experience completely normalized cycles within a few months after discontinuing the Pill. For many even the first post-Pill cycle is normal, including an appropriate thermal shift.

Post-Pill Charting: Begin by following the guidelines for the first and second cycles described in Chapter 6. That is, consider yourself fertile until you can prove otherwise with a thermal shift pattern according to the "3 and 2 and 6" Guideline.

Observing Mucus: Most women experience completely normalized cycles, including a normalized mucus sign, within a few months after discontinuing the Pill. So beginning with the third cycle after discontinuance, you can usually begin charting the mucus according to the guidelines described in Chapter 7.

Still, some women experience continuous mucus for a long time after discontinuance. If this happens to you, just recognize that your body may have been more profoundly affected by the Pill and may take longer to normalize. You will need to rely on the "3 and 2 and 6" Guideline (described in Chapter 6) until your mucus normalizes. There is no need to consult a physician unless the mucus causes itching, swelling, irritation, or has an unpleasant odor.

The Cervical Sign: It is best to wait until after your cycles have normalized before trying to learn the cervical sign. As explained in Chapter 8, the best time to learn is toward the end of a fertile time.

"Cycles" Without Ovulation

An anovulatory "cycle" is one in which ovulation *doesn't* occur. Actually, there will be an ovulation—eventually—but it may be weeks, even months, later than usual. Any bleeding episode that occurs will not have been preceded by a temperature rise. Another way to think of a so-called anovulatory cycle is as a *delayed* ovulation (see chart no. 12.)

So-called anovulatory cycles can occur at any time, although they are very rare between the ages of twenty and forty. Thus, teenage and premenopausal women are the most likely candidates for experiencing "cycles" without ovulation. So are postpartum mothers, especially if they are partially or fully breast-feeding.

Since there is no ovulation, there is no possibility of conceiving during a prolonged period of anovulation. Still, because there is no way to know that a cycle is to be anovulatory until *after* it has passed, you must remain alert to the mucus and cervical signs.

Mucus: Mucus may appear, then disappear, then reappear, almost as if your body were "trying" to ovulate. This "now you see it, now you don't" pattern is natural and often found in such cycles. However, you must consider yourself fertile for three complete dry days after any mucus appearance. If you are also dry throughout the fourth day, you are infertile that evening.

Cervix: If you have incorporated the cervical exam into your fertility awareness experience, be sure to check it each day. If the cervix begins to soften, rise, or open, be alert to the possibility of a pending ovulation.

Temperature and Bleeding: Since there is no ovulation, there will be no temperature rise. However, there may be a bleeding episode, which is usually shorter and lighter than a normal menstrual bleeding. Treat it as a mucus appearance and *consider yourself fertile during any bleeding episode that isn't preceded by a temperature rise.* Fertility continues for four complete dry days *after* the bleeding has ended.

The 21-Day Rule: This rule can be used only by a normally cycling woman. *You must discontinue reliance on the 21-Day Rule for good if you are in your late thirties or early forties and experience an anovulatory cycle.* You are probably entering the premenopause, when cycles can vary so much that the rule is no longer reliable.

If you are around twenty years of age or younger, your cycles may still be normalizing. An occasional anovulatory (or delayed) cycle is not uncommon. (Note: If you have an anovulatory experience at age twenty or younger, you probably began menstruating later than the average female—as late as age sixteen or seventeen.) Once you have records on twelve normal cycles, you may apply the 21-Day Rule.

If you experience an anovulatory (or delayed) cycle *which can be explained by stress,* it is generally safe to return to reliance on the 21-Day Rule once the stress factor is reduced or removed entirely. (See "The Effects of Stress" later in this chapter.)

Stress factors that can cause an anovulatory cycle include:

- Travel (including sudden climate changes)
- Severe emotional stress (including death, escalating marital conflicts, serious problems with children, serious personal, legal, and/or financial problems, etc.)
- Illness
- Sudden weight gain or loss

Infertility: Keep charting your fertility signs—eventually there *will* be an ovulation. After it occurs, use the Postovulatory Infertility Guideline (chapter 7).

Chart No. 13—An Anovulatory Cycle: This is an example of an apparently anovulatory chart. Having used NFP since the birth of the couple's fifth child six and a half years ago, Robin is experienced with the fertility observations. She records all three signs. Notice that Robin and Larry are careful to defer lovemaking for at least four days after every mucus episode.

Most couples who are experienced with the cervical sign would not defer during the four dry days after a mucus observation. Notice that the cervix is low, closed, and firm (+) during those days. But because Larry and Robin feel that it is extra important to avoid pregnancy, they wait for confirmation from all three signs.

There is a bleeding episode (days 30 and 31) which is treated like a mucus patch. Larry and Robin wait until the evening of the fourth dry day after the bleeding before having relations.

Although you don't see it here, the fertility signs unfolded as usual (including a thermal shift) starting on day 49. A genuine menstruation occurred on day 66. The 12 to 16 count-back showed the ovulation occurred sometime between days 51 and 55.

Miscarriage

Nature's solicitude is nowhere more evident than in the processes that unfold right after a miscarriage. Fertility usually returns immediately.

If you wish to take advantage of peak fertility to plan a subsequent pregnancy, watch for the signs of fertility. It is also wise to begin temperature-taking right away. However, don't be surprised if the readings seem high in the beginning. After you conceived, progesterone entered your system to help sustain the pregnancy; after a miscarriage, progesterone levels may descend slowly. Wait a few days for the temperatures to lower and stabilize; they will.

If you wish to postpone conception after a miscarriage, it is best to establish a postovulatory temperature rise according to the "6 and 2 and 3" Guideline before resuming relations. Depending on how advanced you were in your pregnancy, there may be a bleeding after the miscarriage. This bleeding could confuse your normal fertility signs, especially the mucus. If your pregnancy was well advanced—say, twenty weeks or longer—postpartum conditions could exist. In this case use the guidelines for post-childbirth fertility which follow.

Postchildbirth Fertility

The return of fertility depends on whether you are bottle-feeding or using ecological breast-feeding for natural child-spacing (see chapter 10). We will presume in this section that you have elected to bottle-feed or to partially breast-feed (i.e., give some water, express milk from time to time, and/or give some formula feedings). Under these circumstances it is likely that fertility will return very quickly *even while you are breast-feeding*. But under all circumstances you can consider yourself infertile for the first two weeks after childbirth. Thus, lovemaking can be resumed anytime

CHART NO. 13:
An Anovulatory Cycle

PERSONAL FERTILITY CHART

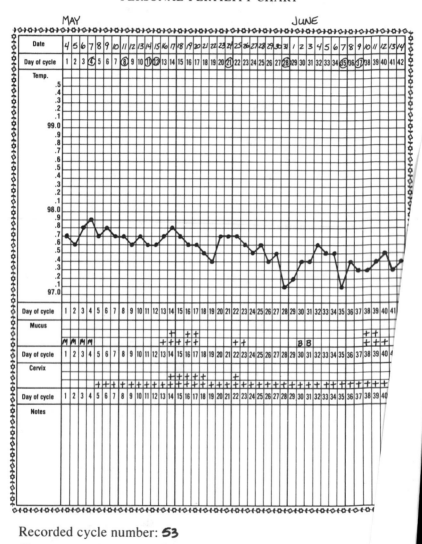

Recorded cycle number: **53**

Shortest previous cycle: **37** days

Number of days in this cycle: **66** days

during this period, depending on the mother's health and comfort.

Beginning with the third postpartum week, charting should be resumed and you must assume fertility until you can prove otherwise. Since mucus may be obscured by the lochia (postbirth bleeding and drainage), temperature is the only sign that can be reliably charted.

Taking Your Temperature: Unless you have help, your sleep is likely to be interrupted during the first several weeks after your baby's birth. Will this affect your temperature readings? Yes, but you should take your temperature anyway.

The best advice is to pick a time when you get the longest period of uninterrupted sleep—say, midnight until 4:00 or 5:00 A.M.— and take your temperature at the same time every day. If there is any kind of change—say, you got less sleep than usual or you ended up taking your temperature much later than usual—take your temperature but make a note about what is different. (Example: "7:00 A.M. temp instead of 4:00 A.M." "Restless night—1 hr. sleep only.")

Never forget: *Some* kind of temperature reading—explanation included—is better than no temperature reading.

Postpartum Fertility: A first postpartum ovulation has been detected as early as twenty-seven days after childbirth, although ovulatory cycles as early as six weeks after childbirth are uncommon. It appears that if a bleeding occurs at about six weeks after the birth, it is not menstrual, but is caused by a possible estrogen withdrawal. In terms of specific figures there is approximately a 95 percent chance that there *wasn't* any prior ovulation if bleeding occurs within forth-two days after childbirth.[1] For the mother who is fully breast-feeding, the chances are nil.

Still, during the postpartum phase, caution is your watchword and charting your beacon. *A couple with urgent reasons to avoid another pregnancy must presume fertility from day 15 postpartum until they observe an unequivocal, sustained rise in the temperature according to the "6 and 2 and 3" Guideline.* To be sure, this requirement may demand quite a bit of abstinence, but it also offers the couple the greatest degree of certainty.

Most couples, however, do not require such a high degree of certainty. Thus, they can follow the usual guidelines as follows:

Mucus Sign: You are fertile on all mucus days plus *three complete dry days* after the mucus has stopped. If the fourth day is also dry, you are infertile by the evening, anytime after 8:00 P.M.

Cervical Sign: Do *not* use the cervical sign unless you have had previous experience with it prior to pregnancy and already know how to recognize the changes. Presume fertility if the cervix shows two-plus sign (+ +) or three-plus sign (+ + +) characteristics.

Breast-Feeding: Any situation that results in decreased feeding (and therefore decreased suckling) may bring on ovulation. Be especially watchful of mucus and cervical changes at these times:

- Discontinuation of night feedings
- Introduction of milk as either supplementary or complementary food
- Introduction of water
- Introduction of solids
- Any alteration of baby's feeding pattern because of sickness, irritability, or a change in household routine (moving, holidays, etc.)

If ovulation has not yet occurred, it is practically guaranteed as the baby weans. Be especially alert to the fertility signs during that time. For complete security consider yourself fertile during the weaning until the temperature rise has been established according to the Postovulatory Infertility Guideline.

Return of Your Cycles: It is impossible to give a definite answer as to when you will return to your usual normal-length cycles. The first ovulatory cycle (as proved by the thermal shift) will probably be a long cycle. The immediately succeeding cycles are also likely to be long. In general, unless you are breast-feeding, you are likely to return to your normal-length cycles gradually, usually within four to six cycles.

The 21-Day Rule: Do not—repeat, do not—rely on the 21-Day Rule until you have experienced six completely normal postpartum cycles. This requirement may mean that after childbirth it will be a year or longer before you can rely on the 21-Day Rule.

Premenopause

At some point, usually between a woman's late forties and her midfifties, the ovaries stop responding to the follicle-stimulating hormone (FSH). This is the menopause, the cessation of the woman's reproductive activity. This phase in a woman's life is also known as the "change of life" and the "climacteric."

Declining Fertility Problems: Since the premenopause can extend over a fairly long period of time, a woman's body adjusts gradually to declining fertility. This may be reflected in the random appearance and disappearance of mucus. Occasionally there may be a bleeding episode. Weeks or months may proceed without a temperature rise, marking a long period of infertility or anovulation (see

" 'Cycles' Without Ovulation" earlier in this chapter). On the other hand, a woman may suddenly experience signs of fertility and regular cycling that go on for months at a time.

Temperature: Temperature-taking at this time will offer you special security. With a daily reading you can be confident that ovulation has *not* taken place even if you haven't menstruated for a long time. If the temperature remains at a high level more than nineteen days following the ovulatory phase, you are very likely pregnant. (See footnote, page 31.) However, statistically, pregnancy is rare.

Bleeding: You may experience bleeding and occasional spotting during the premenopause. *Consider yourself fertile during any bleeding episode unless it follows a sustained temperature rise.* If you have neglected temperature-taking, wait until the evening after four full *dry* days have passed after the bleeding before considering yourself infertile.

If you are concerned about bleeding, or if it increases in quantity or incidence, have your doctor examine you.

Premenopause Guidelines: Because of the special conditions surrounding the premenopause, the guidelines for infertility are modified a bit:

1. You are infertile after a temperature rise according to the Postovulatory Infertility Guideline (chapter 7) through *only* the first three, not five, days of a new cycle. (Reason: Unusually short cycles sometimes occur.)
2. You should *not* use the 21-Day Rule anymore. (Reason: Cycle lengths may become too variable for reliability.)
3. You are infertile during all dry days if they are not part of a four-day count after a mucus patch.

Premenopause Mucus: Dryness tends to prevail for most women during the premenopause. Thus, a couple can express their love coitally throughout most of the premenopause without conception occurring.

Some women, however, experience continuous mucus, although this is very rare. But if it happens to you, it may make it more difficult to evaluate infertility. Observe these guidelines:

1. If you are familiar with, and confident in, the cervical sign, use it to determine infertility. But if in doubt, you're fertile!
2. If you are not familiar with the cervical sign, wait out the mucus for one or two cycles. After that, you may begin to consider yourself infertile on alternate continuous mucus days. But if there is any change to a more fertile mucus, you are fertile! Fertility continues until the evening (after 8:00) of the fourth day past any appearance of such mucus *or* until after an appropriate temperature rise.

Hot Flashes: A typical hot flash occurs suddenly. It affects the upper part of your body, causing the skin to redden, get heated, and sweat. Usually the flash disappears within minutes, although you may experience a number of them throughout a single day and night. The flashes may continue over a period of weeks, disappear for a few weeks, and return.

However annoying, hot flashes have a benefit: On any day or days that you experience hot flashes, your estrogen levels are too low to bring on ovulation. These days may be considered infertile provided, of course, you are *not* experiencing fertile-time mucus.

The Effects of Stress

It appears that both physiological stress (e.g., illness, lack of sleep, sustained periods of heavy exercise) as well as psychological stress (e.g., anxiety, worry, prolonged tension) tend to *delay*—never to induce—ovulation.

Why the delay? We don't know. The effects of stress on a woman's cycle are not completely understood.

What is known is that under physical stress, the body's less essential functions are reduced or even dispensed with entirely so that all energies can be directed toward the survival of the organism as a whole. Because our reproductive function is "less essential," physical stress may cause the body to bypass the physiological requirements of the reproductive organs, causing a temporary suspension of their operation. This may explain why women involved in competitive sports sometimes report a temporary cessation of menstruation. (Also, see the following section, "Changes in Diet and/or Exercise."

Psychological stress is more subtle. It may disturb the subtle "tuning" in the brain hypothalamus and, as a result, may curtail the rise of FSH. Since FSH is the ovulatory "kickoff," none of the other events of the cycle, including ovulation, can unfold in proper sequence if its secretion is curtailed.

If you are under stress—job loss, death in the family, severe marital tensions—your menstrual/postmenstrual phase may last longer than usual. You may also experience no mucus or intermittent mucus patches. (See " 'Cycles' Without Ovulation" earlier in this chapter.) Take it all in stride and carefully observe the Menstrual/Postmenstrual Infertility Guidelines (plus the Mucus Patch Fertility Exception and the Alternate Days Fertility Exception) in chapter 7. Once there is a reduction in the stress you are enduring, your cycles—and your fertility signs—should return to normal.

Changes in Diet and/or Exercise

A change in eating habits, a weight gain or loss, and/or a change in exercise routine may cause a temporary effect on cycles. You could experience a shorter cycle, a longer cycle, or even an anovulatory cycle. This is normal, and normal cycling should resume once your body adjusts to the physical change.

However, it is also possible to stop cycling altogether (the technical word is amenorrhea). In adult women about 22 percent of the total body weight must be fat in order for regular ovulatory cycles to continue. Thus, a woman without any "fat to spare" may experience amenorrhea if she undergoes as little as a seven-to-ten-pound weight loss. This condition is not uncommon among women involved in competitive sports; it invariably affects anorexic women. If you experience amenorrhea, it is wise to consult a physician.

10

❖❁❖❁❖❁❖

How to Space Your Children Naturally by Breast-Feeding

Friends assure me that breast-feeding is an excellent means for avoiding pregnancy. They have tried it and it works.

Other friends insist they have tried breast-feeding to avoid pregnancy and found that it absolutely does not work—and they have the babies to prove it.

So who is right?

Answer: *All* of my friends.

Breast-feeding—what it does and what it cannot do—has been a subject of controversy for the past several decades. It has been only recently that we have come to understand more about its role in human reproduction, especially its role in child-spacing.

Yes, breast-feeding *is* effective in suppressing ovulation for a prolonged period after childbirth, *but only if certain conditions are met*. The conditions are that an infant receive *all* nourishment and water by suckling at the mother's breast. *All* of it. This practice is called complete breast-feeding. It is also known as ecological breast-feeding.

Mothers who practice partial breast-feeding by expressing their milk for a later feeding will *not* enjoy the benefits of a prolonged period of postpartum infertility. Nor will mothers who give their babies occasional supplementary bottles of baby formula or who give them water. Indeed, *any* cutback at all in breast-feeding results in the resumption of normal ovulatory cycling—sometimes as early as three weeks after childbirth!

Special Benefits: By contrast, ecological breast-feeding has several effects: It releases a special hormone called oxytocin that promotes uterine contractions. These lessen to some degree the postbirth bleeding and help the uterus regain normal shape.

Nutritionally, there can be no better food for your baby than breast milk. Studies have shown that in comparison to bottle-fed children, breast-fed babies have:

- Between two and four times fewer incidents of respiratory infections.
- Between five and twenty times less diarrhea.
- Between ten and twenty-two times fewer miscellaneous infections.
- Substantially less asthma, hay fever, and gastrointestinal infections (the latter are the main cause of infant mortality).

But, of course, ecological breast-feeding's most interesting effect is that in some unknown way it suppresses ovulation for many, many months after childbirth. Most couples who avail themselves of ecological breast-feeding have children spaced approximately sixteen to twenty-eight months apart, without giving a moment's thought to birth control.

Special Advantages: This degree of spacing is ideal from many points of view. In "Child-Spacing," a superb article that first appeared in *Child and Family,* Dr. Herbert Ratner, a public health physician and medical editor in Oak Park, Illinois, enumerates some of the advantages. He notes that:

Nature's prescription . . . (1) brings youth to child-bearing and the arduous early child-rearing years, (2) permits children to grow up with more intimately shared lives, (3) closes the generation gap between parent and child, particularly valuable in the adolescent years, (4) lengthens the joys of parenthood and grand-parenthood, (5) allows for leeway in case of obstetrical misfortunes and tragic events, (6) gives parents the opportunity to reexamine their goals while reproductive options are still available, and (7) [permits the couple to] blissfully ignore birth control during the period of greatest sexual activity.*

Frequent breast-feeding has advantages that touch the children of the marriage. Dr. T. Berry Brazelton, a Harvard pediatrician and knowledgeable researcher on infant development, points out that infants and children denied loving contact and communication for months or even weeks at a time risk growing up severely damaged. They may become emotional cripples, even retarded.

With this in mind, it is interesting to note that an integral part of child nurturing involves an infant's need to suckle. Breast-feeding meets not only a child's nutritional needs but also certain emotional and psychological needs. It is because nature considers it so important for a mother to be available to her child for the first year or two that complete breast-feeding signals her body to suspend ovulation for a prolonged period after the baby's birth. This way, baby receives attention, undisturbed within the first year by the equivalent needs of a younger sibling.

Complete Breast-Feeding Practice: When using breast-feeding for purposes of child-spacing, it is essential that your baby have access to your breast *whenever he or she wants it throughout the day and the night.* Here is why:

---

*The article was reprinted in the Spring 1978 issue of the *International Review of Natural Family Planning* and reprints are available for $1.00 postpaid. Write: The Human Life Center, St. John's University, Collegeville, Minn. 56321.

The evidence shows that the suckling action—not the production of milk itself—is what causes the prolonged period of postpartum infertility. For example, experiments with sheep and wallabies have shown that if the teat is surgically denervated, the mother animals are no longer infertile even though the baby animals can continue feeding normally.[1]

In this connection, the breast-feeding practices of the !Kung tribe of the Kalahari Desert in southern Africa have been studied extensively. (The exclamation point denotes a clacking sound that preceeds the pronunciation of the tribal name.) The !Kung do not use contraceptives and do not have cultural practices that tend to regulate fertility, such as late marriage or intercourse taboos during lactation. Still, the average completed family size is 4.7 children and the mean birth interval between children is over four years. "If mortality is taken into account, one can calculate that it will require about 300 years for the population to double,"[2] reports Dr. R. V. Short, who holds an endowed chair in reproductive biology at Monash University in Australia and is chairman of Family Health International at Research Triangle Park in Chapel Hill, North Carolina.

Researchers are convinced that it is breast-feeding that contributes to such long child-spacing intervals. It has been observed that if a !Kung baby should die, which brings a natural end to breast-feeding, the mother is soon pregnant again.

The Importance of Suckling: The considerably longer than usual birth interval among the !Kung seems to be caused by the constant *suckling* by the babies. "Studies by Melvin Konner of Harvard and others have shown that the mother carries the infant wherever she goes and that it sleeps beside her at night," reports Dr. Short. "The infant suckles frequently during the day (about four times per hour), although each feeding lasts for only a minute or two. The infant also suckles frequently at night, even when the mother is sleeping."[3]

Another study in Rwanda, a central African country, showed that there was a substantial difference between the conceptions of rural versus urban babies. At the time of the study, 75 percent of conceptions of urban babies occurred between six and fifteen months postpartum. By contrast, in rural areas 75 percent of the conceptions occurred a minimum of two years later, from twenty-four to twenty-nine months postpartum.

What made the difference?

According to the authors of the study, the breast-feeding patterns were quite different for the rural Rwanda mothers as compared to their urban counterparts. The rural women carried their babies on their backs, allowing them to nurse anytime they wanted, while the urban mothers had less physical contact with their babies and the nursing took place along a more or less regular time schedule. Thus, urban babies suckled less frequently than rural babies, with the result that their mothers became pregnant up to four times earlier than rural mothers.[4]

Quite a different study followed ten bottle-feeding and twenty-seven breast-feeding mothers in Edinburgh, Scotland. On average, the bottle-feeders tended to ovulate eleven weeks postpartum; the breast-feeders, thirty-six weeks postpartum.

Even more significant is the fact that not one of the breast-feeders ovulated if she nursed six or more times a day and for more than a total of sixty minutes daily. Any cutback in this frequency or duration of breast-feeding seemed to be a signal to the body to resume ovulatory activity. It is also noteworthy that the women who ovulated latest of all were the mothers who breast-fed longest (fifty-three weeks), suckled their babies most frequently, continued night feedings longer, and introduced supplementary foods more gradually.[5]

There is a significant point in all these studies: *Any* cutback in suckling (including abandonment of nighttime feeding or any introduction of water and/or supplementary feeding) has been shown to cause resumed ovulatory activity *even though* the mother is still breast-feeding. Dr. Short points out that it is this pattern of less than complete breast-feeding that underscores the belief that breast-feeding isn't reliable as a method of family planning. The fact is that complete breast-feeding is a reliable child-spacing mechanism; partial breast-feeding—which may include supplementary feeding, water, milk expression, even extended periods on a pacifier!—is *not* reliable for child-spacing purposes.

Why suckling acts to inhibit ovulation isn't known with certainty, but Dr. Short has a hypothesis: that suckling sends a message to the hypothalamus through the neural pathways, which results in a decreased secretion of the luteinizing hormone (LH). As you may recall from chapter 2, the LH rise is an ovulatory kickoff. If LH remains suppressed, so does ovulation.

Effectiveness of Breast-Feeding: Ecological breast-feeding to space the birth of children is so effective that an article in the *New England Journal of Medicine* stated that in the world at present breast-feeding "has a larger statistical effect on couple-years protection than currently available technologic contraceptive programs."[6]

The June 1976 issue of the *International Planned Parenthood Federation Medical Bulletin* reported that "lactation world-wide is estimated to prevent more births than all organized family planning programs and thus has a definite contraceptive action."

But while breast-feeding is effective, it is important to restate once again that the effectiveness relies on *two important conditions that must be met:*

1. Your baby must be nourished exclusively at your breast. Not even water should be offered; your milk is all the nourishment and fluid necessary.

2. Nursing should be frequent throughout the day and night, all twenty-four hours. This eliminates even the use of pacifiers to quiet and calm the baby. Suckling quiets and calms babies just as well, with the added advantage of contributing to your infant's emotional well-being.

You may decide to do what many couples do: use breast-feeding for natural child-spacing purposes until you have completed your desired family size. After that, you can begin charting your fertility signs and avoid pregnancy by making love only on infertile days. After all, at least 80 percent of your cycle is infertile!

Tips for Ecological Breast-Feeding: Get off on the right foot: Avoid a medicated childbirth if possible. It is a fact that a medicated childbirth can interfere with an infant's ability to breast-feed. As one doctor expressed it: "These babies always come out floppy." A baby that is still drugged won't be able to nurse properly at first. As a result, sometimes mothers and babies get off to a bad start with the mother losing her confidence in her ability to breast-feed at all.

But don't be discouraged if you do get off to a bad start for the first few days or a week after your baby is born. It happens to many mothers. By the second week after the birth, everything begins to go smoothly and the mothers do remain infertile.

Convenience: One thing you will enjoy is the convenience. Here is what one mother said:

I was prepared for a lot of bother, but I can't believe how easy it is to breast-feed. I remember buying formula, sterilizing bottles, making up the formula, getting up in the middle of cold nights to heat the bottles—not to mention sitting up in the living room feeding the baby. Ugh!

With breast-feeding, the milk is always there, always sterile, and always at precisely the right temperature. Middle-of-the-night feedings are a snap: I just place our baby to my breast and go back to sleep. Now, how can anyone consider that difficult?

Continuing Breast-Feeding: Once breast-feeding begins, let your baby be the leader. When he or she indicates the need for food or even just to nuzzle and suckle, offer your breast. Remember: It is the continuous nuzzling and suckling that is the apparent ovulation inhibitor. Give your infant full rein.

Unless there are urgent reasons to do so, don't force weaning. Let your baby begin eating solids at his or her pace, not yours. Soon enough your infant will want to take food off the table. This could occur at five months; it could occur later. Rest assured that provided your diet is adequate, your milk will provide your baby with all his or her nutritional requirements while breast-feeding continues. Consult your doctor about proper diet and supplements to ensure that your milk provides baby with all needed nutrients.

Prolonged Breast-Feeding: I was surprised by how many mothers continue to breast-feed for years, *literally* for years. One mother has been breast-feeding for nearly two and a half years even though her ovulatory cycles resumed some seventeen months earlier. Why bother? Here is what she said:

> Our baby has become so much a part of my own rhythm that it's no more troublesome to nurse him than it is to have him in our family. It's soothing for both of us and never really interferes. If we're out shopping, we just wait until we get home. In fact, many times he has had to wait, but even at two and a half he understands that. I *like* prolonged breast-feeding. Nursing offers us a quiet, soothing time to share together.

Natural—Not Instinctive: Breast-feeding is *natural* in the sense that there is no interference from technology, but that doesn't necessarily mean that it is *instinctive*. Unless you have been around breast-feeding mothers, you will certainly have your share of questions and will need some answers.

If I had to credit one place for answering the questions of would-be breast-feeders, I would unquestionably salute the La Leche League International. Here is what one new mother told me—a typical story:

> I could never have learned how to breast-feed without the league. I had inverted nipples, plus my milk didn't come in for five full days. I was so worried and had so many questions that I called my chapter leader four and five times a day. I was that desperate.
>
> Imagine trying to call a doctor that often. You just wouldn't. And if your doctor were your only source for breast-feeding information, you wouldn't breast-feed either.

The league also provides excellent books on all manner of subjects related to breast-feeding. There are two that I recommend in particular: *The Womanly Art of Breast Feeding,* which is the league's own book, and *Breast Feeding and Natural Child Spacing,* by Sheila Kippley. The former deals with breast-feeding in general, which for many women actually means partial breast-feeding (milk expression, supplementary bottles, supplementary water, etc.). The second book, as the title suggests, concentrates on the wider meaning of complete or (as some have called it) ecological breast-feeding, including its power par excellence as a child-spacer.

So for information or for detailed *personal* help, contact:

> La Leche League International
> 9616 Minneapolis Ave.
> Franklin Park, Ill. 60131

PART THREE

❖❀❖❀❖❀❖

Fertility Awareness: Unexpected Benefits

11

❖❖❖❖❖❖❖

The Special Advantages of Fertility Awareness for All Women

It will probably begin to happen to you within the first two or three cycles after you learn about the signs of fertility: You will notice *other* things about yourself. "By observing their cycle, some women notice that certain phenomena which they thought were haphazard always recur during the same phase, seeming to indicate a hormonal factor," reports Suzanne Parenteau-Carreau, M.D. "The symptom may be migraine, nausea, itching, acne, increased appetite, weight gain, feelings of distension in the stomach, a special odor, and so on."[1]

There are many other matters that often become uncovered once a woman learns her fertility signs. Often the knowledge is a source of relief. For example, many women who had experienced uncomfortable ovulatory signs thought they signaled health problems. So it was a relief for one woman to learn that the discomfort she felt again and again was ovulatory pain—not the first tentative signs of an impending appendicitis attack. Another woman felt recurrent mild disturbances in the general area of her abdomen.

Another worry laid to rest: She had suspected the onset of bleeding ulcers.

Medical Advantages: Many doctors report medical advantages of fertility awareness. "The first time I had a woman come into my office and tell me that she was twenty-two to twenty-four days pregnant was a real eye-opener to me," a Connecticut physician reported. "I find that NFP mothers come in for prenatal care much sooner than any other group of women. I think this is a real step forward."

Another advantage: Knowing the time of conception can help a doctor manage a difficult pregnancy if complications develop. Sometimes the age of the fetus determines which procedures can or cannot be risked.

Pregnancy aside, women often report vaginal infections almost as soon as they develop. The temporarily confused mucus sign triggers the woman's alertness, bringing her in for a medical examination much sooner. In a few cases learners have been referred to physicians by their teaching couple because the mucus sign indicated possible pathology. More than one case of cervical cancer has been caught in the early curable stage because of NFP awareness.

Peace of Mind: Use of natural family planning can offer relief in unexpected ways. This mother's experience is illuminating:

> One time while we were still using contraceptives, my period was two and a half weeks late. Naturally, I suspected pregnancy. Unfortunately, I had taken strong medication a few weeks before when I had had a bad flu. So for almost three weeks I worried myself sick: Did my medication hurt a developing fetus? I was beside myself until the day menstruation finally began.
>
> But it wasn't until just a few weeks ago that I realized just how different things can be with NFP. My son's leg had to be

X-rayed. The technician was reluctant to allow me to go into the room with my eighteen-month-old baby, since I could possible be pregnant. I just couldn't let my baby go in the room all by himself! I was able to assure the man that I was not pregnant. But before NFP I would have been uncertain and would have taken a chance. Instead, it was a beautiful feeling to be able to enter that room with complete peace of mind.

Fertility awareness gives me the complete control over my reproductive life that I never had before.

Self-awareness: A working woman told me that she takes advantage of the ebb and flow of her cycle to do her job. Tasks requiring sustained concentration and attention—researching and writing major company reports—are scheduled for the first few days of a new cycle and during her ovulatory phases. She has learned that her concentration is best at those times.

In contrast, this woman reports a slight elevation of tension a few days before her menstrual flow begins. Sustained concentration is more difficult. Therefore, these days are reserved for getting rid of nuisance jobs—sending short letters and memos, checking certain facts and figures to be used for future presentations, and the like.

A computer software saleswoman is highly irregular and suffers from cramping, nausea, and physical distress when menstruation begins. This woman keeps track of only one fertility sign: her mucus peak. Reason? She knows that menstruation will follow thirteen days later. Thanks to this important piece of fertility awareness, this woman was able to avoid scheduling either a flight or an appointment with an important customer on day 1 of a new cycle—something that was never possible before she learned to recognize and interpret her mucus sign.

A few years ago a new advantage emerged for this woman. Information became widespread on a new classification of drugs (prostaglandin antagonists) that offer relief from the type of severe menstrual pain that she suffers. She tried the medication—and enjoyed 100 percent relief!

But she still keeps track of her mucus peak because there is one requirement to meet for the medication to be effective: She must begin taking it a minimum of a day and a half *prior* to menstruation. No problem. In every cycle she begins taking her medication 11½ days *after* her mucus peak. (She knows menstruation follows 13 days after the peak. She just subtracts a day and a half from the 13 days, which yields 11½ days.) So for this woman, combining fertility awareness and the right medication has finally left her completely free of any concerns whatsoever about scheduling travel or business appointments.

Of course, fertility awareness is helpful in other areas besides the workplace. A mother of seven recognized that she was too lenient with the children during her ovulatory phases ("*nothing* bothers me then"). She works at striking a balance throughout her cycle.

Couple Relations: Awareness of fertility offers a woman—and a couple—a powerful tool for self-understanding. It can improve relations, as it did for this couple:

> My wife gets irritable for a day or two around the time she ovulates. Since I keep the charts, I know in advance when to expect this. We still have fights, but they're quick, two-minute things. We both know what's behind the flare-up.

Another young couple came to a new understanding about the wife's sexual feelings:

> A few days before menstruation I feel achy and uncomfortable—we both understood this and we never had intercourse. However, there were many other days when I was totally uninterested. It seemed as if I was always making excuses to pass up lovemaking. We were both beginning to wonder if it was something psychological.
>
> After learning the fertility signs, we realized that I feel

uncomfortable during the ovulatory phase. Since I have short cycles—twenty-three to twenty-five days—there are many days per cycle when I have no interest in intercourse.

This awareness has lifted a burden for both of us. We now know our problem was physiological, not psychological. Today we're very comfortable with each other sexually.

Another woman's yearning for a baby was sometimes overwhelming. When she learned NFP, she recognized when those "times" occurred: three or four days during her ovulatory phases. The couple had very serious, urgent reasons for avoiding pregnancy. "But I'm sure that I would have gone ahead with a pregnancy if we had used contraceptives," she reported. "I don't think that I would have been able to help myself." Instead, the recognition that her acute longing for a baby had a hormonal basis—and would pass with the ending of her ovulatory phase—made it far easier to cope with pregnancy avoidance.

There was an unexpected bonus: "My husband now understands what's happening and helps me get through the days when I ache for another little one. He has also developed some lovely ways of making me feeling sexually attractive without allowing me to seduce him. I never expected so much consideration from him and I *never* thought of him as sensitive—but he is."

12

❄❄❄❄❄

Contraception and Natural Family Planning: What the Experts Say

Without abstinence there is no natural family planning.

Abstinence would appear to be the drawback to natural birth control. *But astonishingly, couple after couple have reported that, while sometimes difficult, the required abstinence period has turned out to be another advantage of using natural methods!*

The conclusion was unexpected and surprising, but there had to be something to it. I had had personal, face-to-face interviews with almost 200 men and women and talked to another 45 to 50 individuals by telephone. To learn if the responses would be different with complete anonymity, I sent out approximately 260 six-page essay-type questionnaires, of which 164 were returned. No matter how I sought the information, the overwhelming response was that natural methods were "satisfactory" or "moderately satisfactory" and more often, "highly satisfactory." These ratings were made most often by couples who had used artificial methods (predominantly the Pill) over a long period of time, so they had something to compare it to.

Indeed, despite the abstinence, these couples gave very high ratings to natural family planning and surprisingly low ratings to contraceptives. For example, only 10.6 percent of those who had used contraceptives rated them as "highly satisfactory." In contrast, natural family planning methods were rated "highly satisfactory" by 74.5 percent. On the other end of the scale, 26.1 percent of the respondents considered contraception to be "highly unsatisfactory," but only 1.8 percent of the respondents gave the same low ratings to NFP.*

This apparent high satisfaction rate was sustained when the respondents were asked if they would recommend natural family planning to others. Only 1.2 percent reported that they would not make this recommendation, while a smaller percentage (0.6 percent) reported that *usually* they would not recommend the methods.

In contrast, 89.8 percent of the respondents reported that they would recommend natural family planning to others; 0.6 percent said they would recommend the methods, but with reservations.

Only 0.6 percent of the respondents let the question go unanswered; 7.0 percent were equivocal. They would recommend the methods to some couples, but not to others.

This high satisfaction rate for natural methods corresponds to other statistical evidence:

---

*In fact, a total of 58.8 percent of the respondents rated contraception as having been either moderately unsatisfactory, unsatisfactory, or highly unsatisfactory, whereas a total of only 4.5 percent of this same group gave NFP such low ratings.

Total positive response to contraception—that is, either moderately satisfactory, satisfactory, or highly satisfactory—was 33.4 percent. In contrast, total positive response to natural family planning was 93.5 percent, and, as noted before, 74.5 percent actually rated the natural method as "highly satisfactory." (7.3 percent made no evaluation of contraception and 1.8 percent made no evaluation of NFP).

Note: All figures are rounded and thus do not add up to 100 percent.

Item: A 1969 survey funded by the Nuffield Foundation interviewed 2,179 couples living in Mauritius, an island country in the Indian Ocean. The couples had learned the Temperature Method of natural family planning some seven years previously; researchers wanted to know how many were still using this method variant. Results: 83 percent were still relying on the method seven years later. Only 96 couples (or 4.4 percent) had changed to an artificial method. The rest either had switched to calendar rhythm (2.4 percent) or no longer had any need for birth control (menopause, separation, etc.).[1]

In comparison, family planning researchers have noted that the dropout rate for any artificial method is as high as *50 percent within the first year!*

Item: A two-year study of approximately 1,000 couples in five countries (United States, Colombia, France, Canada, and Mauritius), conducted by Claude A. Lanctôt, Frank J. Rice, and Consuelo Garcia-Devesa under the auspices of Fairfield University in Connecticut, showed that only 4.1 percent had abandoned NFP for either an artificial or a surgical method during the course of the study.[2]

Item: Approximately 10,000 were enrolled in a program in Patna, India, in 1980. A small incentive payment made for a little over a year to attract people into the program was discontinued at the end of 1979. Nevertheless, 95 percent were still using the method a year after incentive payments were discontinued.[3]

Item: A study in England of 410 couples followed over two and a quarter years showed that 74 percent of the husbands and 75 percent of the wives felt that the Temperature Method had helped their marriages. (Only 9 percent of the husbands and 8 percent of the wives felt that it hindered the marital relationship; the rest of the respondents weren't sure.)[4]

Why were satisfaction levels so high? Why were so many couples willing to stick to a method that involves abstinence?

Disequilibrium:
Contraception's Equal Partner

One element becomes most apparent in reading psychological literature concerning contraception: An intrinsic imbalance, or disequilibrium, often exists for couples who use artificial methods. Recognizing this disequilibrium, some researchers attempt to tailor the appropriate contraceptive to the couple, depending on which partner is more or less responsible.

For example, Dr. Charles H. Debrovner, clinical associate professor of obstetrics and gynecology at the New York University School of Medicine, suggests that female-oriented contraceptives such as the Pill and diaphragm are suitable if the woman is able to assume responsibility and isn't subordinate to her husband. In contrast, Dr. Debrovner favors male-oriented artificial contraception—which boils down to condoms—if the husband is more dominant and the wife is unwilling to take responsibility for contraception.[5]

Dr. Peter Barglow, director of psychiatric residency training at Northwestern University Medical School in Chicago, believes that taking contraception out of the woman's control is "risky." Because it is *she* who will be pregnant, presumably the woman will be the one who is more careful in using effective contraceptive measures. In Barglow's opinion, "the only indication for advising a woman to have her partner use the condom is complete inability to use any kind of contraceptive device herself."[6]

Dr. Ruth W. Lidz, who worked with Yale University's Department of Psychiatry until her retirement, makes no bones about the disequilibrium that contraception can foster in the marital relationship. She points out that when partners have grown up in settings where male/female roles are distinct, the marital equilibrium is often upset if the wife handles birth control for the couple. This is especially the case if the man needs to feel dominant; he may actually try to interfere with contraception. On the other hand, assumption of family planning responsibility can be upsetting for some women. They become anxious and uneasy, preferring their husbands to "take the responsibility and control."[7]

One example of disequilibrium is expressed by Dr. Charles V. Ford, adjunct associate professor of psychiatry at the University of California School of Medicine. Dr. Ford writes: "Initially contraceptive choice must include whether or not one wishes to communicate one's intentions to the spouse or the sexual partner."[8] And certainly some modes of birth control are so unilateral (vasectomy, the Pill, tubal ligation) that one *can* ensure that pregnancy does not occur without even revealing one's intentions to a spouse or sexual partner. On the other hand, a woman can also make a unilateral—and private—decision to abandon use of the Pill to achieve a desired pregnancy.

What Couples Say: That contraception tends to engender at least mild disequilibrium came through in reading the questionnaires. A husband whose wife had been on the Pill described what he liked about it: "I didn't have to think."

Another husband reported that the couple had used the condom before switching to natural methods. But his wife also reported use of the diaphragm, foam, and the Pill. Could it be that the wife had been at least partially unwilling to communicate her intentions to her husband? But after thoughtfully reviewing both the question and its answer, I understood the disparity in their answers. The question read: "Were you using any birth control methods (including rhythm or coitus interruptus) prior to changing to NFP? If so, which method (or methods) did you use and for how long?" The man's answer was a model of precision: *he* had used the condom—a perfectly adequate response when "you" in the question is taken as a singular pronoun.

At heart, contraception is a singular affair.

Minor Disequilibrium: The disequilibrium is not always flagrant or persistent. Sometimes it only seems to flare up under certain circumstances. For one woman a vacation experience caused a minor flare:

> I didn't plan too well. Anyway, I ran out of contraceptive jelly for my diaphragm. My husband became extremely annoyed and said, "You should have been better prepared." What he meant was that *I* should have been better prepared to provide for *his* pleasure. *He* shouldn't have to worry about a thing.

A woman with a surprise mini-Pill pregnancy reported a milder version of this disequilibrium:

> Once we got over our bolt-out-of-the-blue astonishment, my husband and I were actually rather pleased that I was pregnant. Still, I remember that when we first got the report, I was left with a feeling that *I* had failed at something that was *my* job.

For some couples, the use of artificial methods may be symptomatic of deeper problems of manipulation, control, and unequal commitment. The following story from a woman now separated from her second husband would seem a case in point:

> I once sat Jack down and really explained to him how much I wanted *us* to have a baby, the two of us. He felt that since we each had children from previous marriages, there was no reason to have any more. I talked to him for nearly three hours, trying to explain to him exactly how much it meant to me. I didn't think he understood a word I said. But I was wrong.

One thing changed after that long talk: All of a sudden he wanted to take charge of our birth control and use a condom. But after only a few weeks we both agreed that neither of us liked it. I went back to the diaphragm. Still, he checked to make sure that I was wearing the contraception at every intercourse. It didn't matter how turned on he was; he always took just a moment to make sure I had it in. It was always in the back of his mind that I might just "forget" to use it, since I wanted a baby so badly.

There were times I didn't feel like having intercourse after "inspection." I never refused him, you understand, but sometimes the checking killed the mood.

As a matter of fact, women's occasional disinterest in engaging in intercourse has been clinically noted by Dr. Lidz. According to Lidz, what seems to be operating is frustration at having sexual intercourse "for no purpose" when contraception is used.[9]

Contraceptives don't always provoke such negative responses. Once women are confident they won't get pregnant (for example, when taking the Pill), many report increase zest for relations, a fact noted by many researchers.

For some, contraceptives provide benefits. One woman said that her husband's willingness to use condoms proved how much he loved and cared for her. He disliked using the prophylactic, but he didn't want to risk his wife's health by use of either the Pill or an IUD. Another husband viewed his wife's use of a diaphragm—with all the messiness and hassle it entailed for her—as a demonstration not only of her love for him but of her concern for their shared physical relationship, since it meant that *he* didn't have to use a condom.

Restoring Equilibrium: Still, the most *equal* relationship is often found among couples using natural methods. There are reasons for this, of course.

First of all, whenever artificial methods are used, usually one partner must absorb most, if not all, of the disturbance they cause. Certainly this is the case with oral contraceptives or the IUD. Only the *woman's* health—even her life—is at risk.

The only male birth control method that seems to pose a health hazard is vasectomy.

Barrier methods, especially foam and diaphragm, are "messy"—something that troubles women considerably more often than men. All barrier methods are, of course, interruptive. Both partners must absorb the disturbance of such interruption to greater or lesser extents. But disequilibrium has again been clinically noted: In one study, researchers found that some "coitus-connected methods" —condom and withdrawal—were discontinued because of objections by the husband. In contrast, there were no objections noted either for the diaphragm or for foam, female-oriented methods.

Like any birth control method, the natural methods do have drawbacks—observing the fertility signs, charting them, coping with abstinence—but the difference is monumental: These drawbacks are *shared*.

13

◇◆◇◆◇◆◇◆◇

Artificial vs. Natural:
How Do They Compare?

Some researchers worry that since natural methods require the willingness to accept mutual responsibility, effectiveness will be reduced. What if there isn't an "equal" sense of responsibility?

This can be a problem, but it isn't unique to natural birth control: Artificial methods are more effective when both man and woman are involved. As a matter of fact, family planning doctors and researchers are beginning to recognize that contraception is more effective when both spouses are interviewed. A joint interview makes the male aware that he, too, plays a role in the couple's birth control; even if it is just a passive role—as is usually the case with artificial methods—it is a *role*.

When men become involved, results are usually better, sometimes dramatically so. In a study in Iran, psychiatrist Iradj Siassi found that only 12 percent of one hundred wives continued to take their oral contraceptives for six months when they were solely responsible. In contrast, an experimental group of one hundred other couples showed a 93 percent compliance rate during the same six months. The difference? In the experimental group, *the husbands* were responsible for dispensing the Pill to their wives each day.[1]

While there may be a cultural element involved here, Dr. Judith Bardwick suggests a critically different dynamic: "If you want to predict the behavior and attitudes of women, then the best single variable is what they perceive are the attitudes and values of the men with whom they are involved. This would be the case even if they were professional and highly educated."[2]

Communication: Agreement to use natural methods does not ensure their success. Another ingredient is required: good communication between the partners.

No birth control method, including artificial ones, is highly effective *unless* the couple can communicate. Two researchers have correlated contraceptive success rates with high communication skills.

Dr. Cornelius B. Bakker and Cameron R. Dightman have found that marital discord can lead to "forgetting" to take the Pill. "Forgetting" also relates to conflicting attitudes toward sexuality—another symptom of inability to communicate and resolve conflict.[3] For example, a wife may feel "used" during the sex act, particularly if her husband refuses to engage in foreplay or makes only perfunctory attempts. Rather than bringing her needs and desires into the open, she may decide to "get something" out of the act of intercourse—in this case, a baby—by "forgetting" to take her Pill.

Unplanned pregnancies are also linked to an inability to create or maintain a satisfying interpersonal relationship. Researchers have noted reasons for this—an echo of Dr. Judith M. Bardwick's observations about abandonment fears: ". . . such an inability may make a woman more dependent upon intercourse as a compensatory strategy for maintaining closeness, or deficiencies in communications skills may make it impossible to discuss clearly and responsibly the issues of contraception."[4]

Maturity: Researchers point out that natural birth control methods have a drawback: They require maturity and stability on the part of both spouses. This is true; this is also true of effective users of contraceptives.

Dr. Peter Barglow has found that women practice contraception much more effectively if they are emotionally mature—a finding ratified by Bakker and Dightman. "Immature women who have a tendency toward acting out and who avoid taking responsibility are prone to forget their contraceptives," they report.[5] Even the ability to tolerate oral contraceptives seems to be related to psychosexual maturity.

One reason teenage unwed pregnancy rates are so high is that the partners not only are manifestly immature but also are unable to perceive reality accurately. The it-can't-happen-to-me syndrome is rampant and reflects an unrealistic evaluation of action and consequences consistent with an immature, even childish, world view.

Impulse gratification—an important measurement of immaturity—is higher in women who have higher rates of unplanned pregnancies. Women who have a capacity to postpone gratification, to delay the satisfaction of impulses, are better candidates for using natural methods. Paradoxically, this capacity is also necessary for women to practice contraception effectively. Artifical birth control may make it possible to satisfy sexual urges immediately, but ironically, the woman who cannot defer sexual pleasure is not a good candidate for effective contraception!

While maturity, good communication skills, and willingness to share responsibility are necessary for effective use of contraceptives, it should be noted that individuals with certain kinds of disturbances will use artificial birth control effectively. For example, a woman with an abnormal fear of pregnancy won't "forget" her contraceptives. Neither will certain kinds of anxious individuals. Extremely dependent women are effective users of artifical methods if their partners want them to be. And the obsessive-compulsive personality type is an ideal candidate for effective contraception.

Other Issues: It has been suggested that natural family planning methods are successful only for couples in committed, *married* relationships. One of the questionnaire respondents made a comment about this:

> I introduced this method to a single friend who leads a fairly active sexual life. She felt that it was a good method for someone who has a steady partner (such as a spouse) because a permanent relationship then exists and the period of abstinence can be dealt with. For someone without such a partner, she felt that NFP would not be a choice method, because the "current partner" may not understand or trust the method and may want to deal with the fertile period by using some artificial method.

While noting the high reliabiltiy of NFP, the Department of Health, Education, and Welfare has listed the commitment aspect of NFP as one of its disadvantages. Notes HEW: "Women who are not committed to a long-term sexual relationship may not be able to have cooperation of a male partner."

Yet Dr. Peter Barglow, among others, has pointed out that married people also tend to use artificial birth control more successfully than unmarried people. One reason for this, according to Dr. Barglow, is that the ability to maintain a prolonged relationship produces a relatively low number of partners. Consequently, the number of exposures to new situations—when one may or may not be prepared with contraceptives—is diminished. "This is consistent with proper planning for the bearing of children. It also correlates with the capacity to do something skillfully over a period of time," Barglow reports.[6] Other researchers point out again and again that unmarried people—and not-just teenagers—are poor users of contraceptives.

The Role of Commitment: The fact that fertility awareness methods can "work" only in a relationship with some commitment may explain why I met so few single people relying on natural birth control. Three singles spoke to me about their use of the methods: one man and two women. In none of the cases did I speak to or meet the respective partners. In contrast to the married couples, none of the three even suggested the idea of my talking to the partner to learn their mate's feelings about using a mutual method.

NFP teachers tell me that occasionally single people come into the classes, but not often as couples. Usually the woman comes unaccompanied. Her motivation: to discontinue the Pill.

When an unmarried couple attends classes together and practices NFP, their relationship often changes very quickly: Either they end their involvement or they become more committed, often marrying.

Becoming more committed, even marrying, is not only related to the growing closeness these methods foster; facing abstinence *together* also helps each partner see the other as a unique, very special individual. And as Dr. Viktor E. Frankl points out, "Grasping the uniqueness of a loved one understandably results in a monogamous partnership. The partner is no longer interchangeable."[7]

There is another element involved—a criticial one—illuminating the vast difference betwen artificial and natural birth control. According to Dr. George E. Maloof, a psychiatrist affiliated with the North San Mateo County Mental Health Center in the San Francisco area, artificial methods "may lock a couple into an arrested state of marital development wherein their feelings are not shared." In such a case the couple's interpersonal problems simply are not confronted. In contrast, natural family planning methods not only enable the couple to share and communicate, *but the methods themselves can actually serve as an aid to that sharing and communication if the couple mutually agree to use them.*

In other words, if you have difficulties talking, sharing, and communicating your feelings, your ambivalence about pregnancy, conflicts about your sexuality, as well as other problems related to your intimate relationship, you may find that the use of natural methods will help you to open up, and to do so *at a rate that can be comfortably accommodated by each of you.*

Deepening Marital Joy: Of course, natural family planning is not solely for couples who have interpersonal difficulties. Indeed, couples who already have a good relationship are usually surprised by how much better it becomes. "We were always a close couple," said a woman married eleven years. "But I can't believe how much closer we've become in the last three years since we started relying on fertility awareness. In fact, my husband told me that he feels we've grown more intimate during the past forty months than during all the previous years of our marriage put together. I agree."

For another couple, the decision to share the responsibility—and cope with the abstinence—brought the spouses closer, deepening their communication:

> My husband was anxious to try anything besides what we were using. He was also ready to make birth control a mutual responsibility.
>
> Despite the fact that I have difficulty abstaining when I'm ovulating, the advantages far outweigh this one hurdle. Perry is aware of this and is very understanding, trying to be more affectionate in other ways. However, we are growing the longer we use the method.

I have to realize that he is trying not to become "turned on" at the wrong time and might even act aloof, forgetting that I need more affection, not less, during abstinence. This is a struggle for us, but one in which we've both become more aware of each other and our feelings and attitudes about sex. We have become closer through the communication we've had to have in order to be successful with this method.

The idea of an ongoing marital romance was expressed to me by many husbands and wives. A nine-year veteran of contraception discussed his experience:

My wife and I have romantic memories of many of our abstinence periods. We have almost no romantic memories attached to the years when Barbara was on the Pill. We have also learned that abstinence isn't always positive unless we really work at it.

A wife married for fifteen years said something along similar lines:

Some of our abstinence times have been funny and wry, others filled with yearning and romance, and a few, just plain dreary. Because of NFP, we are continually writing new chapters to our love story. Some chapters are better than others but we both realize that we would have a very small book if we could make love whenever we wanted.

Another wife's reaction was summed up in a single sentence: "I now know the true meaning of the word 'intimate.'"

The Heart of the Matter: Intimacy is the most important goal of all our deeply held romantic aspirations. Our vulnerability lies in the fact that true intimacy cannot be achieved alone; rather, it depends completely, totally, 100 percent on *another.* Since acceptance of abstinence within the marital bed implies love, trust, and confidence in each other and in a shared future, this may be one reason why many men, and especially women, "blossom" emotionally and sexually after the couple begins to rely on fertility awareness. As the world-famous psychologist and father of self-actualization, Dr. Abraham H. Maslow, has pointed out, "the people who can't love don't get the same kind of thrill out of sex as the people who can love."[8]

There is evidence for Maslow's view in a study published in the *New England Journal of Medicine*. Of one hundred couples described as predominantly happily married, researchers noted that any sexual "difficulties" experienced by the couples "probably reflected interpersonal problems to which both the husband and the wife contributed." The researchers also found that sexual dysfunctions reflected various problems, educational "deficits," conflict within the relationship, inhibitions, and physiological difficulties. They concluded that "it is not the quality of sexual performance but the affective tone of the marriage that determines how most couples perceive the quality of their sexual relations."[9]

The same phenomenon was noted nearly two decades ago by researcher Lee Rainwater. In one study Rainwater found that when there is mutuality in the genital relationship, it is usually accompanied by a deeper satisfaction and security within the marriage.[10]

Do couples using natural family planning methods achieve deeper satisfaction and marital security? Judging from what the couples *say*, it would appear to be the case; judging from what they *do*, the evidence may be overwhelming.

One statistic will summarize what I mean.

One hundred and sixty-four men and women returned my questionnaires. These individuals were a diverse group geographically and had widely different educational, social, and religious backgrounds. (Many respondents specifically pointed out that they were not Catholic, lest I suspect a religious basis for their positive response to NFP.) The couples had only one thing in common: They had learned to use natural family planning methods during or, in the case of a handful of newly married couples, prior to marriage.

The divorce rate for this sampling of married couples was 0.6 percent. In other words, *less than 1 percent of the respondents had been previously married and divorced!* Specifically, only one individual out of 164 who responded had been divorced.

This was a first marriage for 161 respondents; 2 respondents had been previously widowed.

Why such a low divorce rate? What makes the difference? It is difficult to say. One thought that came to mind was that a large percentage of the couples were Catholic. The Roman Catholic Church remains the only major Western religious body that upholds a couple's vow of lifetime fidelity even after civil divorce. This is why Catholics cannot remarry while the first spouse is living. (An exception is made if a church-recognized annulment is granted. This is a declaration by a Tribunal to the Church that a marriage never legally existed as a sacramental union according to Canon Law.)

But even if all the respondents were Catholic—which they were not—the explanation is weak. Writing in the June 1978 issue of *U.S. Catholic,* Monsignor Steven J. Kelleher reported: "There are at least six million divorced Catholics in the United States; almost half of them have remarried. The proportion of divorces among Catholics is approximately the same as that among Jews and Protestants: from one-third to one-half of all marriages."

Another explanation for the low divorce rate is the possibility that the marriages were only a few years old. One expects that most couples can tough it out for at least a *few* years.

Unfortunately, not even that answer will wash: only 30 percent of the couples had been married six years or less; 40 percent had been married between six and eleven years;

30 percent had been married eleven years or more. *Thus, 70 percent of the couples represented had been married six years or longer.*

Several proponents of natural family planning have suggested that the growing divorce rate is related to widespread use of contraceptives. Whether this is true or not, certainly it cannot be argued that improved contraception has *reduced* the divorce rate.

Back around the turn of the century only one in twenty marriages in the United States ended in divorce. Between 1915 and 1920 the rate doubled to two in twenty marriages and then remained fairly stable at that rate until the mid-1960s, when a dramatic change began. A report published in the July-August 1982 issue of *Family Planning Perspectives* showed that about one-fifth of the children whose parents married *before* 1960 lived through a separation or divorce of their parents as compared to almost two-fifths of the children whose parents married *after* 1966. The investigators categorized this nearly twofold increase of family disruptions within such a short time period as "remarkable."

Sociologists, psychologists, psychiatrists, marriage and family counselors all have different theories to explain this phenomenon. Still, one significant change beginning in 1960 that *didn't* improve matrimonial longevity was the much-heralded arrival of the contraceptive Pill on the U.S. market.

Thus, the low divorce rate in my sample gives apparent support to the thesis that there is a link between the widespread use of contraception and divorce—except for one problem: The majority of the respondents had used artificial birth control at one time in their marriage. Moreover, some kind of self-selection is involved in changing to NFP. Spouses in a deeply troubled marriage who are completely unable to communicate are not likely candidates even for learning, much less for using, natural family planning.

Still, this datum reveals . . . something. One thing is certain: Use of natural family planning is not harmful to a couple's relationship. But other questions are less certain: Can natural family planning improve marriages? Increase marital and family happiness? Could it be a significant factor contributing to the permanence of a marriage?

While the answers to these questions are less certain, I remember something said by James B. McDaniel, Jr., M.D., a staff member of the Buffalo Planned Parenthood Center in Buffalo, New York. Speaking of a method that involves periodic abstinence, Dr. McDaniel said, ". . . it is based on some of the finest qualities in man, namely, self-restraint, discipline, and responsibility.

Indeed, the qualities required to build a lasting marriage.

14

❖❖❖❖❖❖❖

The Surprising News About Abstinence

Because it requires mutual coping, abstinence has turned into a bonus for all but a handful of couples. Indeed, the self-denial, discipline, and mutual sharing and decision-making involved in natural family planning have been a spur for both individual and mutual growth. A husband married for fifteen years commented on this:

> In the beginning we thought that if my wife went on the Pill, the freedom of having intercourse as often as we wanted would bring us closer together. . . . But now that we are using NFP, our marriage is growing better every day. It didn't on the Pill. We've learned that there is more to marriage than sex.

Couple after couple have indicated that their relationships have become more intimate, have deepened. But very few expected such positive, apparently unrelated rewards when they first set aside contraceptives, especially the couples who came to NFP classes out of desperation. One couple enrolled because the wife couldn't tolerate the Pill and needed emergency surgery for an IUD-related complication. The couple signed up for a course in natural family planning as a last resort. "When we learned how long the abstinence could be, it was a shock," the husband told me. "I said to my wife, 'Honey, we're never going to make it on this method.' After four months I guess it's getting a little better, but it hasn't gotten easier. Maybe in another year or two I'll feel differently."

Very likely the man *will* feel differently in another year or two, according to Don and Sylvia Kramer, directors of the Twin Cities Natural Family Planning Center at North Memorial Medical Center in Minneapolis. The Kramers, too, came to NFP when there was nothing left. They had used calendar rhythm and all the major artificial methods—IUD, Pill, diaphragm—without any great degree of satisfaction. The only thing left was natural family planning.

Through their own experience the Kramers recognized that there are usually five stages in learning to cope with abstinence—the same five that Dr. Elisabeth Kubler-Ross identified for terminally ill patients dealing with their impending deaths. This may appear to be a bizarre comparison, but there are similarities: Both are essentially *life struggle* situations. These five stages represent the normal human response to such situations, regardless of what form they take in our lives.

The Five Stages: This is how the stages often unfold with respect to abstinence:

Stage 1—Denial. "Honey, we're never going to make it on this method" is the first stage. The feeling is that it *can't* be; that abstinence isn't *really* necessary, that there *must* be a way out. In other words, the reality is denied. When the couple accepts the fact that abstinence *is* part of natural family planning, they may then move into the second stage.

Stage 2—Anger. The couple may lash out at each other and argue about other things, but their anger really stems from the feeling of being "conned" into use of a method that has such restrictions. One or both partners may feel this anger to differing degrees. Generally, the anger disappears when the couple thinks they have found a way out; they have moved into stage 3.

Stage 3—Bargaining. The couple begins to accept the reality of the situation by trying to find ways to make it easier. "Okay, we've got to abstain. Let's see if we can shorten the days."

Sometimes the couple consults the chart together and discusses "taking chances." They may also decide to try using contraceptive barriers during the fertile time. This type of solution, however, makes the couple more acutely aware that intercourse isn't natural. Something is off, not right, missing. Couples previously on the Pill who enjoyed intercourse without any barriers find readjustment to artificial barrier methods too disheartening. And, of course, some couples using barrier methods during the fertile time are surprised by an unplanned pregnancy. So once a couple realizes there are no viable "bargains," they move into stage 4.

Stage 4—Depression. "Okay, we'll abstain. Abstinence never lasts *too* long, after all. There is always an end to it. It's really not that bad." Not exactly *empty* words, but hardly a cheering thought. And depression sets in. After all, it is hard—very hard—to be content with such a trying situation. At this point the couple is usually ready to move into the last stage.

Stage 5—Acceptance. It would seem that this stage is the best. But it is neither best nor worst; neither a happy stage nor an unhappy one. It just *is*. Both completely accept that they have a mutual responsibility and "job" to share with respect to family planning.

Growth Potential: Of course, the job isn't necessarily an easy one. "It is important that couples practicing periodic abstinence not delude themselves that they are not experiencing deprivation," reports psychiatrist Abraham J. Twerski, M.D., director of the Gateway Rehabilitation Center in Pittsburgh. "This delusion could result in noxious repression and pathologic defenses."[1] Dr. Twerski also notes that recognition of the deprivation will allow the couple to develop more healthful methods of coping.

Indeed, frank admission of the difficulties of abstinence linked to a willingness to develop appropriate coping mechanisms offers a couple great potential for growth. There are many reasons for this. Internationally renowned psychiatrist Dr. Viktor E. Frankl has pointed out in *The Unheard Cry for Meaning* that when we are no longer able to change *a situation,* we are challenged to change *ourselves.* If this challenge is accepted, we rise above ourselves, becoming more than we have ever been.[2] In a word, we have *grown.* Indeed, this is what happens to the couple who accepts abstinence. *They can't change the situation, but they have the opportunity to act as partners in a growth process that inevitably accompanies the use of natural family planning methods, if the couple truly accepts the partnership.*

Of course, no one experiences these stages in exactly the same way. It takes months, sometimes years, for most couples to move from denial to acceptance. But some couples can move from denial to acceptance in one evening. Others skip several stages altogether; for example, they may start bargaining the first night they learn about natural family planning and never bother to deny or get angry. There are also couples who are beyond bargaining; they're already too depressed.

Individual spouses aren't necessarily at the same stage at the same time. A husband can be angry and his wife depressed; a wife may be interested in bargaining while her husband has reached acceptance. The experience of the three following couples reflects acceptance of the deprivation caused by abstinence and growth through the stages:

> We are in the process of writing a book which we hope will be helpful to other couples. In it we describe our personal struggle from viewing abstinence as a burden, to coping with it, to acceptance of it as being positive, to making it a creative part of our marriage, to becoming joyous about it! We have grown so much and to a great extent we believe that much of it has been because of NFP.

> When we first started using the method there was that longing for Phase III; now we are realizing a great happiness even during the abstinence. . . . How super it is to run up to my husband and give him a big hug when he walks toward the house each evening. I feel like a young bride when I prepare one of his favorite meals and take walks in the new snow in the evenings followed by cuddling up in bed with a great feeling of being loved even though we are in a short time of abstinence. I always thought, "Well, life will begin when we reach the OK part of the cycle," but now I realize that life is special every day of the cycle.[3]

> Our desire for intercourse is at its highest level during the most fertile days. It is nearly impossible for us to refrain on these days, but we are learning to manage. We used withdrawal—and I got pregnant with it once—but today we no longer use withdrawal at all.
>
> The effects on our marriage have been good. Initially, my husband said that we would try NFP for six months and then we'd make a decision about whether or not to continue. NFP has forced us to communicate. This area has always been weak with us. We "grew up" so to speak by taking responsibility for our drives. The methods are highly satisfactory and I'd recommend them to other couples.

The Natural Birth Control Disequilibrium

It would be a pleasure to report that every couple passes more or less smoothly through the five stages to acceptance, but it would be far from the truth. For some troubled couples, natural family planning can become a fresh battleground in the marital fray. A wife described what happened in her marriage:

> My husband did not want to be "told when to have intercourse." So usually when I told him that it was safe, he would begin *his* period of abstinence. He was not going to be forced to make love by the calendar; he was not going to be used as my sex object.

This woman went on to write in her questionnaire that her husband didn't want to use condoms because they were too disruptive. "But I also refused to use a diaphragm because I felt it would be too disruptive," she added. "I feel about the diaphragm the way he feels about a condom." The woman also felt that the Pill and the IUD were hazardous. Moreover, she was convinced that there was just something "right" about a natural method. "It makes sense to me that NFP allows one to be in touch with one's cycle, and without contraceptive barriers a couple is truly two-in-one."

But the husband's questionnaire revealed that he saw no advantage to natural methods; he thought that NFP was "unsafe" and that it killed spontaneity. He rated the method "unsatisfactory," would not recommend it to other couples, and felt that the effects had been negative.

It was a no-win situation: The wife had reached acceptance, but the husband remained angry. Despite the woman's misgivings and deepest wishes, the couple relied on a female-oriented barrier method during the fertile time. As far as the wife was concerned, it was the only way to achieve a measure of peace in the marriage.

I received a letter from a wife who also reported negative effects on her marriage:

> My husband feels that we should not be using a method that limits his freedom of sexual expression. He has gone along with the method only because I can't tolerate the Pill anymore. But during abstinence times he is sulky and unpleasant. NFP has solved my medical problem, but it has created a marital problem that I don't know how to solve.

Dr. Max Levin, a neuropsychiatrist and clinical professor at New York Medical College, commented at length about such situations in an issue of *Child and Family:*

> When a man and wife are unhappily married, the smallest thing can loom up as a big problem. . . . In such a marriage periodic continence can become a major issue. The husband regards sex not as something he can give his wife, but as something he can give *himself* as compensation for his various grievances.
>
> In my own experience there has been no exception; in the cases I have seen where periodic continence was presented as an intolerable burden, there has not been a single case where I didn't find something seriously wrong with the marriage. There was no love, no spirit of devotion. One or both partners were immature, egocentric, selfish. They were wrapped up in themselves, not in each other. It was not the frustration of the . . . method that was disturbing them [and they don't] need to use other contraceptive methods. They need therapy and counseling to find out what is wrong with their personalities and why the promise of their marriage has not been realized.[4]

Manipulation and Control: Natural family planning can be used negatively: Manipulation and control problems are not strangers to NFP couples. They are at the root of this wife's comments:

> I guess my husband viewed me as the "victor" because we did not use contraceptives during four years in which we had

two pregnancies. On the other hand, I felt he was the "victor" and a very effective fighter. We might not use contraceptives, but we had sex when *he* was willing. Using NFP unilaterally really set me up: I was damned if I did and damned if I didn't. My husband took *no responsibility* in this area; any mistakes or pregnancies were my "fault" (to use his choice of words).

It is not surprising that the woman's husband took no responsibility for the couple's family planning. It is symptomatic of severe disequilibrium that one partner—usually the wife—is left fielding the family planning responsibility alone.

But not always! The issue of control is at the heart of this wife's complaint:

I wonder how many letters you receive from women who find that NFP works *too* well? For over a year now, I've been anxious to begin another pregnancy. Unfortunately, my husband has been more hesitant . . . and NFP has helped *him* get his way. The total effectiveness of NFP has resulted in a very frustrating year for me, and my *husband* is controlling our fertility to a greater extent than I am.

Minor Disequilibrium: Severe disequilibrium is usually symptomatic of other difficulties in the relationship. But even good relationships can be uneven in a different way:

Long abstinence periods cause tension. During our short safe times I initiate sex oftener than I'd like because I know I'd better do it before the long abstinence.

Another woman felt that her husband didn't trust her "calculations" yet, "possibly because I am so unsure of myself." This disturbance is likely to clear up with time, since the couple is new to NFP and is learning it in one of the most difficult circumstances: the lactation period after childbirth. As time goes on, perhaps the husband will become more involved in the "calculations"—to use the wife's word—and will become a true partner in the decision-making about fertility and infertility.

In another marriage it was clear that the partners did not view fertility as a *shared* condition:

> Let me say first that there seem to be little resentments in marriage toward personalities or things said or done in the past. On top of that, I think that my husband holds me or my body responsible for his not being able to have sex. I feel frustrated not only at that responsibility but also for our not having sex. In addition, there are those *other* resentments underlying our talks or arguments when we're ostensibly talking about our frustrated sex problems.
>
> For example, he wants to play around during our unsafe periods more than I want to. Then *other* problems or setbacks make him more aware of his sexual frustrations. As a result, we're sometimes having more than one argument in one fight— if that makes sense. In other words, we're ostensibly arguing about sex, but what's *really* causing the resentment is something that happened way back in our marriage.

Sometimes there is difficulty using natural family planning for the simplest, plainest, and most basic reason of all: Abstinence is hard! One husband put it bluntly: "I'm too horny."

A letter from a young wife underscored the difficulty of abstinence:

> Although we will never go back to any other type of birth control, involvement with NFP is not a happily-ever-after story. It is sacrifice and a lot of self-control. After using the Pill, I'm still in the "mind-set" of "if it feels good, do it." It's like going on a diet after pills used to keep me slim.
>
> And what do other women do with husbands that are pushy, don't trust the method, become angry at the wife for not being infertile, then are overly afraid of getting the wife pregnant? What about husbands who are generally frustrated because of lack of sex?
>
> We've got all of the strains, and seemingly little of the enrichment, although there is some. If you catch us during the infertile time, we will possibly be more enthusiastic about NFP. Rationally, it does have everything else beat by a mile.

The woman's feelings about using natural family planning are neither usual nor unusual. Still, as you will read in the next two chapters, NFP can make a big difference in enhancing a couple's intimacy and closeness.

15

❀❁❀❁❀❁❀

Why Abstinence
Makes a Difference

It was a cliché of the early artificial birth control movement that if a couple could physically express their love at will, they would grow closer, strengthening their marriage. Given the soaring divorce rate over the subsequent decades, that promise seems not to have been realized. In contrast, many couples insist that it *has* been realized with a method that involves periodic abstinence. These comments are typical:

> I went through many kinds of pills, experiencing vomiting, migraines, irritation, dissatisfaction. I also felt used—an object used for sex. The memories of us and our marriage were not pleasant, and when we went on NFP, both we and our marriage improved. We tend to think our earlier problems were related to our birth control.

> The ever-present opportunity to have sex became a performance pressure that neither of us enjoyed. At the same time, we didn't feel close enough to talk about what was bothering each of us. We drifted apart. Our prayers became lonely ones—each of us had the attitude that God should help the other to change.

As a first step exploring the value of abstinence, it is important to probe a sensitive area: Why do we make love in the first place?

Why We Make Love: University of Michigan psychologist Dr. Judith M. Bardwick examined some of the reasons for lovemaking. In one study women were asked specifically: "Why do you make love?"

Initial responses were more or less as expected. In other words, the women offered what they considered to be the "right" answers. But after some delicate probing, the researchers learned that all was not quite the way the women had first reported it.

Sex was rarely described as pleasurable in its own right. Instead, two responses were most common: First, sex was a way to demonstrate love in a relationship that the women hoped was mutual; second, if the woman withheld sexual favors, the man would leave. "The fear of abandonment was the single most critical conscious fear," reports Dr. Bardwick.[1] Because this fear was so high, many women perceived a man's willingness just to hold her, without having intercourse, as a sign of love.

This theme was clear in most of my interviews. Many women specifically mentioned how much it meant to them that their husbands were willing to abstain for the sake of their mutual goals. This came out in the questionnaire responses as well. "Strange as it may seem," one woman wrote, "the abstinence has had a positive effect on our marriage. I feel that my husband has to love me deeply in order to abstain." Another woman said: "I feel so secure and loved. My spouse loves me for *me* and not as a sex/bed partner. I know this because during our abstinence, he is still loving and faithful and has self-control."

Mutual Commitment: This woman's comment touches on another fear noted by Dr. Bardwick: Women fear that commitment to the relationship is not equal. Thus, for many women a husband's willingness to abstain is proof of his love and devotion. One young wife, aged twenty-one, had a direct experience with her husband's loving devotion:

> After my little girl's birth, I experienced a lot of breakthrough bleeding that made us abstain for weeks. During this period my husband and I supported each other a lot. Without his understanding, determination, *love,* and willpower, NFP would not have been part of our daily lives. We are very happy to be part of NFP.

But is the woman's husband equally happy "to be part of NFP"? Apparently yes. The husband, aged twenty-five, rated the method as "highly satisfactory" and noted that "it has made us closer and has shifted the emphasis of physical love to a more mature and rounded love for each other."

Other husbands reported themselves pleased by the mutuality, closeness, sharing, and equality that are an intrinsic part of the commitment to natural family planning.

> We've become much closer in our love because of this shared responsibility.

> Since using natural methods I feel more of the power and responsibility of sex, since both of us know exactly when to have or avoid sex in order to have or avoid having children.

> Natural methods offer us a greater knowledge of ourselves and each other and make our fertility as a couple a joint responsibility.

Wives, too, are thrilled to have their husbands "on board" as committed equals in family planning:

> It's neat to feel that my husband is involved in birth control with me and it's not just me popping a Pill, or whatever.

Both share. My husband does the charting and makes sure I've taken my temperature.

I know my husband feels that NFP is highly satisfactory because he's so enthusiastic about it. He's always updating his knowledge, taking my temperature, charting, and helping me to interpret. Sometimes the abstinence period gets me down, but my husband has the ability to really get me through it and into the infertile phase. *He* makes the method worthwhile.

Problem Marriages: If abstinence is helpful for couples who have no marital difficulties, it can also be a boon for those who do. Since most marriages have difficult periods, abstinence can be a sign of commitment that makes it easier for the couple to deal with real issues, real problems. A twenty-four-year-old wife married for four years wrote:

> Abstinence seems to highlight certain problems in our marriage. But if we had not learned to use NFP, I believe that these problems would have been unidentified, remained under the surface, and would have ended up causing more difficulties.

Sexual Disequilibrium: Some couples have problems bringing sexual drives and needs into sync. Often the wife is less interested in frequent relations. But interestingly, even when this is the case, the acceptance of the "ban" can be fruitful for both partners, as one husband discovered:

> Before using NFP, I spent many evenings thinking about how I was going to convince Joyce to have intercourse that night. Meanwhile, she was thinking about how she was going to convince me that we *didn't* need it that night.
>
> Now that we're using NFP, many nights are spent discussing problem areas in our marriage—ourselves, the children, etc. Overall, I would never trade NFP for any artificial method because it has helped us together. I'm also relieved that my wife is not in any medical danger from side effects of the Pill.

A nineteen-year-old wife was also relieved from sexual pressure by the intercourse ban:

> We are both very open about the fact that I don't seem to want intercourse as much as he does, although I am definitely beginning to want it much more than I used to. This pleases both of us. The fact that I can't have it some of the times makes sex all the more enticing, but neither of us thinks that I'll ever be as horny as Lenny. We joke about how grateful I am that we use NFP because the abstinence lasts longer than a headache.

The woman's twenty-year-old husband said that he found abstinence somewhat difficult, "but if the alternative is the Pill or an IUD, we'll abstain." This couple had used condoms ("bargained" with the method) during the first two months of the marriage. However, there were serious reasons for avoiding pregnancy: He was still in school; they had no savings whatsoever; and two intercourses in which they failed to use the condom frightened them. If they continued to "play around" with the method, they might have an unplanned pregnancy. The husband also felt that having played it "both ways"—without abstinence, then with it—the "honeymoon" effect of renewing the physical relationship made for a more exciting, meaningful experience than "sex on demand." He acknowledged that abstinence is hard, but noted that "if it weren't difficult, having intercourse again wouldn't be so exciting either. It's hard to have it both ways."

Thus, for this young couple, the wife's need for less sex was equalized by the husband's need for more sex via the impartial intermediary of their choice of birth control. Neither spouse felt an imposition; the wife enjoyed a respite and her husband found the respite ultimately worthwhile.

Sexual Dysfunction: While natural birth control can be helpful when there are no problems in the bedroom other than unequal desire, it is sometimes most helpful when there are problems of sexual dysfunction. Indeed, it has become a sex therapy cliché that the way to achieve a normal sexual act is to forbid it, while encouraging greater physical intimacy—touching, caressing, fondling—over a period of days or even weeks. Dysfunctions like primary and secondary impotence and premature ejaculation have been helped by the well-known technique of refraining from intercourse, though not from touching.

Implicitly, NFP encourages couples to explore nongenital, nonorgasmic means of expressing affection and love during the fertile phase. One wife said that this "mini-sex therapy" became the inadvertent "cure" for her husband's impotence:

> Things got so bad that I stayed on the Pill despite serious headaches. We felt that it was important that if he could get and sustain an erection, there should be no need for an interruption that could ruin it. That canceled out any barrier methods.
>
> Today we realize that our thinking placed Joe under an intolerable strain. He felt constantly pressured to produce an erection to please me, especially since I was having so many problems with the Pill.
>
> But finally the problems with the Pill became too great. If he managed an erection, I had a screaming migraine.
>
> Matters have improved now that we can't have intercourse for almost two weeks. In fact, we almost didn't make it through the first abstinence phase, which astonished both of us. We bought condoms for the second one, but they created the old problem again: My husband felt the pressure to please me. Everything fizzled, pun intended.
>
> Today we're not having as much intercourse as I would like, but I do enjoy the petting and touching. He does too. I also enjoy the fact that we're not always concentrating on *his* erection, *his* penetration, and whether or not *he* can keep going. Intercourse works out most of the time without our thinking about it—although we still have our flops.
>
> I think that we both accept the reality of the situation,

especially since things have improved over the past thirty-eight months that we've used NFP. My husband has become more accepting of his sexuality and his problems. I have too.

Another couple didn't wish to detail what their sexual problem (or problems) had been, but they found that fertility awareness helped them with the difficulty:

> NFP has definitely been a help to certain physical problems in our marriage and has also helped our relationship. Sex used to be *the* subject in our marriage and created a lot of pressure. Now it's back to a more supportive position. Also, when sex was *the* subject, it wasn't very good. Now that it's more in the background, it's much, much better. NFP has freed us to be more comfortable with sex and each other. Now we're more open and talk about things more, especially since the performance pressure is off.

Sex Is Better: None of the couples I interviewed complained that abstinence had hurt the marriage. A few individuals made this complaint in the questionnaires, as noted in the previous chapter, but most reported that the short abstinence period renewed their zest. One young husband made an interesting comment when asked about the drawbacks of NFP:

> The first and only "drawback" I can think of is the abstinence period. But after having used the method for twenty-two months, I can honestly say that the sexual tension created by the abstinence period is healthy and contributes to deeper sexual love between me and my spouse during the infertile phase.

A wife reported that abstinence restored romance:

> At certain times my husband tends to treat me more specially—like a fiancée rather than a wife. He doesn't take me quite so much for granted, like a cookie he can have anytime. I believe in some ways that abstinence keeps his mind from wandering to other women because he's anxious to have

intercourse just with me. I respond to that by keeping up my appearance; I also make sure that my personality remains appealing to him.

It isn't just that abstinence whets the appetite. Others report that having learned fertility awareness, they feel more confident, relaxed, and responsive, since they're sure that conception can't occur. This is a reaction more common to women, although many men also report it.

Extending Foreplay: Many women derive much greater enjoyment from sexual relations when foreplay lasts longer. Men, too, find that extending foreplay can make the final orgasmic experience more explosive, more enjoyable. Thus, abstinence offers a double advantage for some: It builds excitement and tension *and* extends the foreplay, not only physically but mentally. These comments are typical:

> My husband and I are much more affectionate and open, and we communicate better. Having intercourse isn't just something that happens at bedtime. We build up to it after a whole evening of togetherness.

> I used to think that I liked spontaneity. My wife and I have discovered that lovemaking is actually better when both plan and yearn for sex.

> Abstinence sharpens or rekindles my wife's attractiveness to me and prompts demonstrations of love and affection that I probably would neglect.

> We've both enjoyed the courtship during the time of abstinence and it's fun to prepare for the honeymoon when abstinence is over.

I didn't like being Mrs. Availability the way I was with the Pill. There's a lot more mystery now with the abstinence. I like having the mystery—and believe it or not, so does my husband.

Dr. Donn Byrne points out that imagination is a vital element in sexual responsiveness.[2] Writing in *How Can a Man and a Woman Be Friends?* Mary Rosera Joyce points out that if the human stimulus-response reflex is developed into a stimulus-*reflection*-response process, the main sexual organ, the brain, becomes activated. When this happens, the human sexual experience has the potential to become greater, more all-encompassing. According to Joyce, "The spontaneity of sex is meant to be like the spontaneity of the fine arts, not like the impulsiveness of the child 'playing' the piano."[3]

The best insurance for this variety of spontaneity is *thought*. This bonus of the imaginative faculty is not as readily available to the couple that relies on contraceptives.

I received insight on this matter from one couple who tried to impose an abstinence period on themselves while the wife was on the Pill. "The abstinence just got shorter and shorter and finally didn't exist at all," said the husband. "Sex became boring, and even though we both knew what was happening, we found that we just didn't have the motivation to abstain since we really didn't have to." Now that the couple are using natural family planning, they *do* have to abstain. And they have succeeded. "It makes all the difference," the husband admitted.

The Interpersonal Relationship

While many couples are surprised to find that their sexual relationship improves once they begin relying on natural family planning, an even bigger surprise may be what happens to their *interpersonal* relationship. There is a reason for this: Once a couple mutually agree to use NFP, fertility awareness tends to uncover many matters that might have gone unnoticed, even undiscovered, by the spouses.

A wife described how the change to NFP helped her open better communications pathways:

> When we started using the methods, we really had to discuss a lot of new things. At first I wasn't sure how to interpret the changes in my mucus. We discussed that. Soon we were discussing how seriously we really wanted to forestall pregnancy. This came up especially during the times when abstinence was particularly difficult for one of us or both of us. In fact, we discussed the abstinence problem very extensively— how to cope creatively with the sexual tensions. We also planned how to enjoy intercourse after the abstinence period and our physical relationship took on a special excitement. We had never talked about things so intimately, so personally, or in such detail until we started using natural birth control.

The communication that develops can cover anything and everything: your sexuality, conflicts, goals, your marriage, your children, finances, other problems. Sometimes subtle things like attitudes and feelings that might otherwise have remained hidden emerge.

A husband described how the couple's early difficulties helped him overcome his narrowness vis-à-vis sexual expression:

> My wife wanted and needed more physical affection during the abstinence. I just didn't see any point in hugging or kissing if it wasn't going to lead to something. During those first two years on the method, there were plenty of tears and explosions at our house because of my 'all or nothing' view of sex. That's changed because *I've* changed. I've grown.

One couple made a discovery about sexual attitudes:

> The biggest surprise to me was the fact that *my wife* found the abstinence terribly difficult. I thought that I would have the

problems—but I mean it: I practically had to tie her down to her side of the bed. She also became more aggressive as the abstinence came to an end and she let me know that she was looking forward to having intercourse again.

I was terribly flattered to realize that my wife enjoyed relations with me so much. For years I have been grateful to her for always responding to my "request" for intercourse. But after twenty-eight months of using natural methods, we finally see intercourse as something that we share and give to each other. She gives to me; I give to her.

It is important to discover that the wife is not the sole "giver of gifts." It is an awareness that places both partners on an equal footing.

Another couple made a different discovery about equality and responsibility in the first few years after they changed to fertility awareness methods:

> There were many times when I'd feel affectionate and loving and want to hug and kiss Jenny, or just give her a squeeze. But she'd freeze me out.
>
> Finally I said to her: "Okay, what's going on? What have I done? Why am I getting the big freeze?" You know what her answer was? That we were supposed to be abstaining! "Hey," I told her, "I'm in this too, you know. *I* know that we could get pregnant; I won't let anything get out of hand."
>
> Well, she knew that intellectually, but she still couldn't relax and trust me. Also, she didn't want us to get the least bit excited sexually because she worried about control—specifically *my* control. We worked out that problem for nearly three years. But now she trusts completely that I can—and will— handle our abstinence.

While this wife learned to trust her husband more within their marital relationship, she recognized that her earlier need to maintain their abstinence related to the fact that she had handled the couple's family planning responsibility for so long that she continued to feel responsible. The disequilibrium fostered by *her* prior use of the diaphragm and the

Pill carried over when the couple changed to mutual family planning: She felt solely responsible for ensuring its effectiveness.

Growth Adventure: Of course many couples consider the abstinence quite enough "shared responsibility," but other couples go much further. In many cases the husband becomes intimately involved with the task of charting, even handling it completely. Indeed, one of the most impressive aspects of NFP involves the process of continual growth in the area of *mutual* responsibility—something that is quite distinct from individual responsibility.

One husband said that when he first heard about natural methods he was sure that they would be effective. Then he added: "However, I misunderstood my role. My wife had too much responsibility." The man's comment is indicative of a change from viewing family planning as "her" responsibility to viewing the responsibility as "ours."

The wife's questionnaire revealed more detail about this responsibility and the couple's growth:

> When we first started using NFP, my husband left everything up to me, including maintaining the abstinence, while sometimes trying to encourage me to "break the fast." I told him that I didn't mind "keeping the records" but that we both had to work at maintaining abstinence, and *not* by keeping at opposite ends of the house.
>
> It was after that that we began to work at NFP together. I suppose this new closeness has been gradual, because I cannot tell you exactly when it began, but we are so much more open with each other and better able to communicate.

Total Sharing: The mutuality involved in using fertility awareness can be so profound that it may subtly affect the thinking of a couple. It comes down to this: Men and women stop thinking of themselves as the "opposite" sex; they begin considering themselves the "complementary" sex. This change of thinking was revealed in a small but very important change in language—a fact I discovered accidentally during personal interviews.

The subject of planning a pregnancy came up many times. I tended to direct this kind of discussion toward the woman—a reflection of my own culturally conditioned bias. But during one interview a husband told me about the couple's decision to use NFP to conceive and said, "The first time we tried it, it worked! We got pregnant."

We got pregnant. The phraseology jarred me. But a few interviews later, another husband mentioned that "we got pregnant." There it was again!

Having noted this phraseology crop up twice accidentally, I looked for it deliberately. When I could, I directed questions about the decision to conceive toward the husbands. Seventeen husbands used the plural form of that pronoun in connection with conception. That makes a total of nineteen husbands thinking in the plural about pregnancy, about 20 percent of the men interviewed.

What is more, I had already interviewed over a quarter of the couples before I noticed the two "we got pregnant" phrases used by husbands. As I already mentioned, because of my own bias, I had previously been directing all such questions to the women. I am convinced that if I had caught on sooner, I would have had a larger tally.

At heart, fertility awareness is a completely shared venture.

A Family Affair

The sharing that is involved in fertility awareness affects the entire family. Dr. Mary Ella Robertson, a sociologist who served on the Secretary's Advisory Committee on Population Affairs, U.S. Department of Health, Education, and Welfare, reports that the deeper bond of mutuality and commitment fostered between parents by their use of NFP ". . . not only dramatically improves the marital relationship, but also makes it easier to rear the children. It is a subtle thing, but it's a very real thing: The children sense the commitment of the parents to each other and to them. It enhances the child's feeling that he or she belongs to a united family, one permeated by caring and love."

Other matters are uncovered. For example, the parental dialogue about sex is often made considerably easier. A mother told me her learning experience:

> My parents found it very hard to talk to me about sex. I found out everything from my cousins, not from my parents. But I'm not much different from my mother: I, too, find it difficult to talk to my children about sex. But the simple fact that we rely on NFP forces me and Bob to talk about sex and sexuality a great deal. I found that our discussions over the years have made me so comfortable with the subject that it has been easier than I would have ever expected for me to talk to my daughters about the changes in their bodies and what they mean. Even Bob has said that he feels surprisingly at ease when the girls ask him birds-and-the-bees questions. We both agree that this comfortable openness comes from the fact that we've grown to be completely uninhibited with each other about sex.

Teenage Sex: A mother found that NFP offered a realistic way to discuss premarital sex with her seventeen-year-old son:

> One night my youngest son was talking to me about his girlfriend. To my astonishment, he was actually wondering out loud whether or not he should sleep with her. I don't know what surprised me more: that he was considering it—or that he was *telling* me that he was considering it.
>
> But suddenly I knew just how I felt about premarital sex: I wanted my son's first sexual intercourse to take place under circumstances of mutual love and total commitment. That's

how his father and I had had our first experience—on our wedding night.

I also realized why it had been so hard to deal with the subject with our oldest children. We had used the Pill, so it was fine for *us* to say, "Wait until you get married." The message was: "Don't have sex now; then after you get married, you can have all you want."

Now that we're using natural family planning, the message is different: "You can't have intercourse anytime you please. Look at us: We're married and even *we* can't have intercourse whenever we want. And I know what you mean: Sometimes it's very hard holding off. I can really sympathize with you because Dad and I deal with the problem all the time."

What this mother discovered is that she and her husband are in equilibrium not only with each other but with their children. There were no "Don't you dare!" harangues; instead, there was a communality, a feeling of "I know it's a problem for you because it sure is a problem for us."

In addition, the mother was able to help her son to deal with one of the important challenges of growing up: learning to develop a "deferred gratification pattern." In other words, learning to be responsible on the basis of principle, rather than impulse.

The "instant gratification syndrome"—getting whatever you want as soon as you want it—is the hallmark of the immature person. "Contraception [and] sterilization naturally reinforce the instant gratification syndrome," reports R. J. Hunegar. "NFP reinforces the deferred gratification pattern. Both are viewed as possible solutions for couples needing to avoid pregnancy, but only NFP bears within itself the essential challenge to be consistent in sexuality with what one needs in life as a whole for personal maturity."[4]

A grade-schooler's mother had a rewarding experience in communicating the idea of personal maturity in the arena of sex and family planning:

Danny came home from fifth grade one day having received the school's mandatory sex lecture, complete with a full description of all the contraceptive paraphernalia that's available. I was *very* annoyed: I had wanted his sex education to come from us. Anyway, home he arrived, bright with this brand-new knowledge. Suddenly he asked me if I could tell him what Daddy and I use for birth control.

It was the first time in my life that I was completely relieved that I wasn't on the Pill. I was able to tell my son that Daddy and I don't use anything; that if we want to have intercourse during a time of the month that I could get pregnant, why, we just wait a week or two until I can't get pregnant anymore. Then when we *do* want to get pregnant, we wait for that time of the month when we're fertile.

Danny was very impressed by all of this. He told me that that's the method he wants to use when he gets married, and that he'll wait until his wife is fertile when they want a baby. But when they have to postpone pregnancy, they'll wait for the infertile time.

Already at age ten he's thinking in terms of mutual responsibility for sexual intercourse and family planning.

This kind of thinking is a splendid gift for a mother-in-law to give to a future daughter-in-law.

16

σ⊹σ⊹σ⊹σ⊹σ

Achieving
Sexual Freedom

One question puzzled me during the hundreds of interviews that I conducted: How did the couples begin to use a natural method in the first place?

Answers ran the gamut. Typically, couples told me that they used the method because it posed no health hazard to either partner. I was also told that it was more "ecological" and suitable to couples interested in a "natural" life-style. A few couples cited the fact that natural family planning conformed to their moral and/or religious beliefs.

In fact, I knew that none of these reasons was sufficient. Using calendar rhythm satisfies these requirements, yet almost all the couples had previously rejected that particular hazard-free, "natural," and nonobjectionable birth control measure. Moreover, I recognized that virtually none of the couples interviewed would still be using natural family planning if they experienced surprise pregnancies. So I concluded that a critical requirement influencing the choice of any birth control method is that it be *reliable*.

But even this brought up another question: Why were the couples willing to give this new, essentially "untried and unproved" method a chance? Even then, natural family planning was not well known in the United States—and still isn't. Its reliability is unpublicized, little recognized, and usually confused with the discouraging figures associated with calendar rhythm. Indeed, many women told me that their gynecologists derided their decision to rely on a natural method, assuring them that they would be back in their offices "soon" for prenatal care.

So why, in the face of so little support, did couples risk a natural method? I often asked the question bluntly, but didn't receive satisfactory answers. Later I modified the question by asking why the couple hadn't opted for one of the barrier methods instead of NFP when they came off the Pill. That particular question struck most individuals as jarring. "It's not as nice" was a frequent response. "It's unromantic," "It's messy," were others. And, of course, "We did—and got pregnant" came up occasionally.

I concluded triumphantly that only two important indexes were involved in a couple's choice of birth control: The method had to be simultaneously effective *and* free of interruption. I considered "proof" the fact that women were willing to tolerate such an incredible array of Pill symptoms *rather* than switch to a barrier method.

I also believed that Pill side effects were another reason couples found natural family planning so satisfactory: Selective abstinence can be difficult, but it is certainly more tolerable than many of the persistent physical side effects suffered by many Pill users. (Curiously, few women in my sampling had used an IUD.) And, of course, the benefits of the method were considerable: high effectiveness without interruption of the sex act.

Today I realized that I was far off the mark.

My early conclusion reflected a rather "technological" view of human fertility. I completely overlooked an important, indeed a critical, aspect of human sexuality: the procreative function. Failure to recognize the importance of this function is tantamount to a failure to perceive an individual's humanity and personhood. I am particularly indebted to Dr. Ruth W. Lidz, clinical professor of psychiatry at Yale University School of Medicine until her retirement, for valuable insights into this matter.[1]

Dr. Lidz reports that because the use of effective contraception involves the almost complete and certain frustration of a woman's procreative function, her general comfort, well-being, and self-esteem may be negatively influenced. It may also lead to a variety of symptoms, including depression.

Why such negative reactions? What causes them? Lidz notes several factors that may be involved.

One, of course, is the fact that fertility is a part of a woman's sexuality. This explains why virtually every woman is ambivalent about pregnancy at some time and some women are always ambivalent. Over the years a woman learns to adjust to this. Moreover, she can fantasize about possible pregnancy if she uses less effective contraceptive measures (diaphragm, condom, and others).

In contrast, the effective artificial and surgical methods destroy that necessary ambivalence completely. Worse, pregnancy fantasies can no longer be sustained. In effect, a woman must adjust to the notion of sterility—a notion that is not congenial to many women and may negatively affect self-image and self-esteem.

Other studies indicate that the notion of fertility is very important to women. One group, studying the emotional adjustment of women who had been sterilized, found a striking correlation between successful adjustment and the presence of the unrealistic fantasy that pregnancy was still possible. Another study observed conscious pregnancy fantasies, symptoms, or signs several months after sterilization in 152 women out of a series of 190.[2]

After having described this research in a lecture, I was

told by one woman that the information had, at last, illuminated a situation in her own life. Here is what she said:

> My friend Amy calls me every single month and says she's *sure* she's pregnant. We have the same conversation every month: I remind her that it's impossible for her to be pregnant since she has been sterilized for nearly three years. She ignores that. She tells me that she thinks that the operation must have failed because she's *sure* she's pregnant. Then I remind her that that's what she said last month . . . and the month before that . . . and that she has suspected a pregnancy each month since her operation. But Amy always says the same thing: that *this* time her pregnancy signs are more pronounced.

Amy's persistent pregnancy fantasies are pathetic and sad, but her story helped me to understand why natural methods satisfy on a deeper level. I have come to realize that *whether it is conscious or not*, couples know that a natural method preserves the partners' sense of wholeness. This is because neither partner's fertility is suppressed in any way. And while a couple may choose to avoid pregnancy, they are not at the same time subverting either spouse's fertility. On the contrary, their joint fertility is not only recognized for the powerful force that it is, but it also receives deference and respect from *both* husband and wife.

The woman receives particular benefits. One is that she can preserve that pregnancy ambivalence. She just has to remind herself—and women *do* remind themselves—that the couple can choose to achieve a pregnancy at any time.

Dr. Lidz also points out that a conflict between wanting to be fertile and not wanting a child can be great. This is true, of course, and use of natural methods helps a woman realistically deal with her feelings and share them with her mate. Furthermore, natural methods prevent further emotional conflict caused by deliberate fertility suppression.

There is another fascinating aspect of natural family planning: Use of natural methods requires both planning and a high degree of future-orientation from both husband and wife. This kind of future planning has helped some couples come to grips with their unconscious feelings that there was something "wrong" with sex. This fact was discovered when couples recognized that the idea of planning for intercourse was vaguely disturbing. Before, when intercourse "just happened," as it did, for example, when the woman was on the Pill, these individuals were able to "blame" sudden passions, spousal demands, whatever, for "what happened." Whether they recognized the fact or not, these individuals were not sexually liberated.

Once these couples changed to natural family planning and began to cope with the fact that intercourse had to be deferred *and planned for,* they had to deal with deeper sexual feelings—negative ones—and begin the struggle to conquer them. But even more important, these individuals were *helped by their mates* to achieve sexual liberation. This is yet another example of how the communication and sharing fostered by natural methods can help overcome sexual problems.

Once negative views were confronted, then coped with in a committed, loving, future-oriented relationship, these individuals were ultimately able to enjoy intercourse more than ever before in their lives. So there is a paradox: The apparent "restrictions" of the method played a key role in freeing many individuals from unconscious negative feelings about sex and sexuality. Indeed, the restrictions themselves made the sexual freedom possible.

But it isn't only negative attitudes toward sex that are uncovered. Sometimes the attitudes toward sex are apparently positive, but actually pathological. One wife found that abstinence was difficult for her because she had what she later came to call an "intercourse dependency." In the absence of frequent lovemaking, she felt sexually undesirable and unattractive. It was a real step forward for her in terms of her self-esteem when she realized that she was loved *for herself,* independent of her desirability as a sex partner. It was a lesson she could have learned only through the abstinence requirement of NFP.

Many husbands have learned that there is more to sex than genital intercourse—a hard-won lesson for some men, many of whom were surprised to learn how much they really enjoyed the gentle kissing, caressing, and holding that can be a part of a positive abstinence expression. The move beyond goal-oriented sex—that is, intercourse and orgasm—is a move toward growth.

Surely, natural family planning has many more positive advantages. These remain to be explored. At this writing the methods are so new that little research or exploration has taken place, and there are still many questions.

Many individuals have told me that the change to NFP improved their self-esteem and at the same time deepened mutual respect. As one woman said, "I never realized how much my husband loved me until he threw away my Pills and made me go with him to our first class." Another woman said, "I never thought that Hal would be able to abstain for two days much less for almost two weeks. I guess I didn't think much of him either."

That may be one of natural family planning's greatest contributions: the fact that it encourages some of the finest qualities in ourselves—and in our mates—to blossom.

Using the Personal Fertility Chart

ひとひとひとひ

You may discover that your normal basal body temperature range always begins below 97.0°, the lowest temperature on the chart that follows. If this happens to you, simply change the numbers on your chart so that 97.0° becomes 96.0°, 98.0° becomes 97.0°, 99.0° becomes 98.0°, and chart as usual.

Ordering Additional Charts: The charts in this book are reduced by almost a third of their normal size. You may feel comfortable using them, but many women prefer the full-size, 8½″ × 11″ charts, which are printed in light blue on white paper. (Charting entries, temperature rises, etc., stand out better when the chart is a pale color.)

The cost of the charts (postage included) is:

$4.00—1 year supply
$6.00—2 year supply

Add $1.00 for shipping outside the United States.

All orders must be pre-paid by personal check or money order, made payable to KM Associates. Order from:

KM Associates
P.O. Box 71041
Chevy Chase, MD 20813-1041

Date																																										
Day of cycle	1	2	3	4	5	6	7	8	9	10	11	12	13	14	15	16	17	18	19	20	21	22	23	24	25	26	27	28	29	30	31	32	33	34	35	36	37	38	39	40	41	42

Temp.
.5
.4
.3
.2
.1
99.0
.9
.8
.7
.6
.5
.4
.3
.2
.1
98.0
.9
.8
.7
.6
.5
.4
.3
.2
.1
97.0

Day of cycle	1	2	3	4	5	6	7	8	9	10	11	12	13	14	15	16	17	18	19	20	21	22	23	24	25	26	27	28	29	30	31	32	33	34	35	36	37	38	39	40	41	42
Mucus																																										

Day of cycle	1	2	3	4	5	6	7	8	9	10	11	12	13	14	15	16	17	18	19	20	21	22	23	24	25	26	27	28	29	30	31	32	33	34	35	36	37	38	39	40	41	42
Cervix																																											

Day of cycle	1	2	3	4	5	6	7	8	9	10	11	12	13	14	15	16	17	18	19	20	21	22	23	24	25	26	27	28	29	30	31	32	33	34	35	36	37	38	39	40	41	42
Notes																																											

Recorded cycle number: ____

Shortest previous cycle: ____ days

Number of days in this cycle: ____ days

Appendix

❖❖❖❖❖❖❖❖

Resource Guide for Personal Instruction and Further Reading in Natural Family Planning

The Couple to Couple League provides NFP instruction throughout the United States and a mail-order book service. For information send a self-addressed stamped envelope to:

> Couple to Couple League
> P.O. Box 11084
> Cincinnati, Ohio 45211

The Human Life Center (HLC) will refer you to instruction near you. In addition, the HLC book service offers a range of materials on NFP and related topics. For either, send a self-addressed stamped envelope (business size).

HLC also publishes the *International Review of Natural Family Planning*, a quarterly providing up-to-date scholarly research on NFP plus related subjects. Annual subscription: $15 ($19 foreign). Payment must accompany order.

The Human Life Center
St. John's University
Collegeville, Minn. 56321

An NFP resource is the *The NFP Reader,* a bimonthly newsletter listing new published information and short articles. Annual subscription: $15. (Add $5 for airmail.) The address:

K M Associates
P.O. Box 71041
Chevy Chase, MD 20813-1041

Child and Family, a quarterly magazine, carries articles on child rearing and nurturing, breast-feeding, natural child-spacing, NFP, etc. 1 year: $4; 2 years: $7; 3 years: $10.

Child and Family
Box 508
Oak Park, Ill. 60303

In Canada, for NFP instruction and information, write:

SERENA Canada
55 Parkdale
Ottawa, Ontario, K1Y 1E5

Notes

◊✛◊✛◊✛◊✛◊

CHAPTER 1

1. Robert A. Hatcher, M.D., Felicia Guest, Felicia Stewart, M.D., Gary K. Stewart, M.D., James Trussell, and Erica Frank, *Contraceptive Technology, 1984–1985* (New York: Irvington Publishers, 1984), p. 98.
2. *Ibid.,* p. 221.

CHAPTER 3

1. Gerhard K. Doering, *Proceedings of a Research Conference on Natural Family Planning,* ed. W. A. Uricchio (Washington, D.C.: The Human Life Foundation, 1972), p. 172; "Biology of Fertility Control by Periodic Abstinence," WHO Scientific Group, World Health Organization Technical Report Series, no. 360 (Geneva, 1967), p. 18.
2. Doering, *Proceedings,* pp. 175–76.
3. J. Marshall, *The Infertile Period* (Baltimore, Md.: Helicon Press, 1967), p. 74.
4. Rudolf F. Vollman, "Assessment of the Fertile and Sterile Phases of the Menstrual Cycle," *International Review of Natural Family Planning* 1, no. 1 (Spring 1977): 43.
5. Excerpta Medica International Congress Series No. 224, Advances in Planned Parenthood VI, Proceedings of the VIII Annual Meeting of the American Association of Planned Parenthood Physicians, Boston, Mass., April 9–10, 1970.
6. Josef Roetzer, *Fine Points of the Sympto-Thermic Method of Natural Family Planning,* no. 2 (Tokyo: Japan Human Life Foundation, Oct. 1977), p. 16.
7. Josef Roetzer and E. Keefe, *Fine Points of the Sympto-Thermic Method of Natural Family Planning* (Collegeville, Minn.: The Human Life Center, April 1977), p. 4.
8. John and Sheila Kippley, *The Art of Natural Family Planning,* 3d ed. (Cincinnati, Ohio: The Couple to Couple League International, 1984), pp. 128–29.
9. Josef Roetzer, "The Sympto-Thermal Method: Ten Years of Change," *Linacre Quarterly* 45, no. 4 (Nov. 1978): 370.
10. Edward F. Keefe, "Self-observation of the Cervix to Distinguish Days of Possible Fertility," *Bulletin of the Sloane Hospital for Women* 8, no. 4 (Dec. 1962): 129–36; Edward F. Keefe, "Cephalad

Shift of the Cervix Uteri: Sign of the Fertile Time in Women," *International Review of Natural Family Planning* 1, no. 1 (Spring 1977): 55–60.

11. John F. Kippley, "The Cervix Symptom of Fertility: A Comparative Study," *International Review of Natural Family Planning* 6, no. 3 (Fall 1982): 272.

12. Suzanne Parenteau-Carreau, M.D., "The Sympto-Thermal Methods," *International Journal of Fertility* 26 (1981): 175.

13. Ronald L. Kleinman, M.B., Ch.B., d. (Oest.) R.C.O.G., "Side-Effects," *Periodic Abstinence for Family Planning* (London: International Planned Parenthood Federation, 1983), pp. 44–46.

14. R. H. Gray, "Aged Gametes, Adverse Pregnancy Outcomes and Natural Family Planning: An Epidemiologic Review" (Unpublished paper, The Johns Hopkins University School of Hygiene & Public Health 1985), p. 8.

15. Gabriel Bialy, personal communication to Marianne Rahilly, executive director of the Natural Family Planning Center of Southwestern Michigan.

16. Michael B. Bracken and Kathy Vita, "Frequency of Non-Hormonal Contraception Around Conception and Association with Congenital Malformations in Offspring," *American Journal of Epidemiology* 117, no. 3 (1983): p. 289.

17. F. W. Oescheli, "Studies of the Consequences of Contraceptive Failure: Final Report" (Unpublished paper, University of California, 1976).

18. Hatcher, et al., "Fertility Awareness Methods," *Contraceptive Technology,* p. 153.

19. Kleinman, "Side-Effects," p. 46.

CHAPTER 4

1. Barbara Grizzuti Harrison, "Does Sex Appeal to Women?" *Mademoiselle,* June 1985, p. 102.

2. Abraham J. Twerski, "Psychosocial Aspect of Natural Family Planning," *International Review of Natural Family Planning* 3, no. 4 (Winter 1979): 328.

CHAPTER 7

1. Roetzer, "Sympto-Thermal Method," p. 369.

CHAPTER 8

1. Roetzer, *Family Planning the Natural Way* (Old Tappan, New Jersey: Fleming H. Revell, 1981), p. 99.

CHAPTER 9

1. Kippley and Kippley, *Natural Family Planning,* p. 133.

CHAPTER 10

1. R. V. Short, "Breast Feeding," *Scientific American* 250, no. 4 (April 1984): 36.
2. *Ibid.*
3. *Ibid.*
4. Monique Bonte, Emmanuel Akingeneye, Mathias Gashkamba, Etienne Mbarutso, and Marc Nolens, "Influence of the Socio-Economic Level on the Conception Rate During Lactation," *International Journal of Fertility* 1974, pp. 97–102, cited in Kippley and Kippley, *Natural Family Planning,* 3d ed., p. 200.
5. Short, "Breast Feeding," pp. 36–38.
6. D. B. Jelliffe and E. F. P. Jelliffe, "Breast Is Best: Modern Meanings," *New England Journal of Medicine,* Oct. 27, 1977, p. 913.

CHAPTER 11

1. Parenteau-Carreau, "Sympto-Thermal Methods," p. 176.

CHAPTER 12

1. William A. Uricchio and Mary Kay Williams, "The Mauritius Program," *Proceedings of a Research Conference on Natural Family Planning* (Washington, D.C.: The Human Life Center, 1973), p. 247.
2. Frank J. Rice, Ph.D., Claude A. Lanctôt, M.D., M.P.H., and Consuelo Garcia-Devesa, Ph.D., "The Effectiveness of the Sympto-Thermal Method of Natural Family Planning: An International Study" (Paper presented at the Scientific Congress held in conjunction with the First General Assembly of the International Federation for Family Life Promotion, Cali, Colombia, June 22–29, 1977).
3. The Hong Kong Catholic Marriage Advisory Council, "A One-Sided View of Natural Family Planning," *International Review of Natural Family Planning* 7, no. 1 (Spring 1983): 63.
4. John Marshall, M.D., and Beverley Rowe, M.A., "Psychologic Aspects of the Basal Body Temperature Method of Regulating Births," *Fertility and Sterility,* Jan. 1970, p. 17.
5. Charles H. Debrovner, M.D., "Medical, Psychological, and Social Aspects of Contraceptive Choice," *Medical Aspects of Human Sexuality,* July 1976, p. 33.
6. Peter Barglow, M.D., "Emotional Factors in Contraception," Ortho Panel, Apr. 1973, p. 17.
7. Ruth W. Lidz, M.D., "Psychological Factors in Contraceptive Failure" (Unpublished paper), pp. 9–10.

8. Charles V. Ford, M.D., "Psychological Factors Influencing the Choice of Contraceptive Method," *Medical Aspects of Human Sexuality,* Jan. 1978, p. 91.
9. Ruth W. Lidz, M.D., "Patient Motivation in Selection and Acceptance of Contraception," Mack Symposium, Wayne State University, Detroit, Mich., Oct. 1973. Also published in *Regulation of Human Fertility* (Detroit, Mich.: Wayne State University Press, 1976).

CHAPTER 13

1. Iradj Siassi, M.D., "The Psychiatrist's Role in Family Planning," *American Journal of Psychiatry,* July 1972, p. 52.
2. Judith M. Bardwick, "Psychodynamics of Contraception with Particular Reference to Rhythm," *Proceedings of a Research Conference on Natural Family Planning* (Washington, D.C.: The Human Life Center, 1973), p. 212.
3. Cornelius B. Bakker, M.D., and Cameron R. Dightman, B.S., "Psychological Factors in Fertility Control," *Fertility and Sterility* 15, no. 5 (Sept.-Oct., 1964): 566.
4. B. Kay Campbell and Dean C. Barnlund, "Communication Patterns and Problems in Pregnancy," *American Journal of Orthopsychiatry,* Jan. 1977, p. 135.
5. Bakker and Dightman, "Fertility Control," p. 566.
6. Barglow, "Emotional Factors," p. 17.
7. Viktor E. Frankl, *The Unheard Cry for Meaning (New York: Simon & Schuster, 1978),* p. 81.
8. Abraham H. Maslow, *Religion, Values, and Peak-Experiences* (Columbus, Ohio: Ohio State University Press, 1964), p. 105.
9. Ellen Frank, M.S., Carol Anderson, M.S.W., and Debra Rubinstein, M.S., "Frequency of Sexual Dysfunction in 'Normal' Couples," *New England Journal of Medicine* 299, no. 3 (Jan. 1978): 115.
10. Lee Rainwater, *And the Poor Get Children* (New York: Quadrangle Books, 1960), p. 96.

CHAPTER 14

1. Twerski, "Natural Family Planning," p. 327.
2. Frankl, *Meaning,* pp. 39–40.
3. *The CCL News,* 4, no. 5 (Mar.-Apr. 1978): 5.
4. Max Levin, M.D., "Sexual Fulfillment in the Couple Practicing Rhythm," *Child and Family* 8, no. 1 (Winter 1969): 10.

CHAPTER 15

1. Bardwick, "Psychodynamics of Contraception," p. 197.

2. Donn Byrne, Ph.D., "A Pregnant Pause in the Sexual Revolution," *Psychology Today,* July 1977, p. 68.
3. Mary Rosera Joyce, *How Can a Man and Woman Be Friends?* (Collegeville, Minn.: The Liturgical Press, 1977), p. 41.
4. R. J. Hunegar, "Natural Family Planning—A Way of Life," *International Review of Natural Family Planning* 6, no. 3 (Fall 1982): 288.

CHAPTER 16

1. Ruth W. Lidz, M.D., "Emotional Factors in the Success of Contraception," *Fertility and Sterility* 20, no. 5 (Sept.-Oct. 1969): 761. Also see "Conflicts Between Fertility and Infertility," to be published in *The Woman as a Patient,* ed. C. Nadelson and M. Notman (New York: Plenum Publishing Corp.).
2. David A. Rodgers and Frederick J. Ziegler, "Psychological Reactions to Surgical Contraception," *Psychological Perspectives on Population,* ed. James T. Fawcett (New York: Basic Books, 1973), pp. 306–25.

Index